THE FAMILY AND THE POLITICAL SELF

Having children is one of the most common goals among human beings. *The Family and the Political Self* aims to capture the insights that can be gleaned from taking this truth seriously. One insight is that human beings may not be as self-interested as is commonly supposed. In this book, Laurence Thomas argues that the best construal of the political self reflects this conception of human beings.

Laurence Thomas is professor of philosophy and professor of political science in the Maxwell School of Citizenship and Public Affairs at Syracuse University.

D1564916

THE FAMILY AND THE POLITICAL SELF

Laurence Thomas

Syracuse University

CAMBRIDGE
UNIVERSITY PRESS

CAMBRIDGE UNIVERSITY PRESS
Cambridge, New York, Melbourne, Madrid, Cape Town, Singapore, São Paulo

Cambridge University Press
40 West 20th Street, New York, NY 10011-4211, USA

www.cambridge.org
Information on this title: www.cambridge.org/9780521854177

First published 2006

Printed in the United States of America

A catalog record for this publication is available from the British Library.

Library of Congress Cataloging in Publication Data

Thomas, Laurence
The family and the political self / Laurence Thomas.
p.   cm.
Includes bibliographical references and index.
ISBN 0-521-85417-2 (hardback) – ISBN 0-521-67011-X (pbk.)
1. Self-esteem.   2. Parent and child.   3. Family.   4. Child development.
5. Conduct of life.   I. Title.
BJ1533.S3T48   2005
306.85'01 – dc22   2005008115

ISBN-13   978-0-521-85417-7 hardback
ISBN-10   0-521-85417-2 hardback

ISBN-13   978-0-521-67011-1 paperback
ISBN-10   0-521-67011-X paperback

For Thomas Nagel

A Bridge Over Troubled Waters

Contents

Acknowledgments

Caveat preemptor. Although this book is profoundly inspired by the great French philosopher Jean-Jacques Rousseau, I have not aimed to offer a reading of his political thought. However, I have always been impressed by his thought that there is a sublime excellence that comes about only when human beings interact in the right way (*De L'État de Nature*, sect. 8, para. 2). This claim is generally regarded as the lynchpin of his argument for the move from the State of Nature to Civil Society. If this claim is true, then it follows that human beings are quintessentially social creatures. That is, if the Good is to be attained, it is only through social interaction that we can do so. My aim in this book, then, has been simply to sketch an account of how this might be so. If there is one theme more than any other that holds sway in this work, it is that human beings are not as driven by self-interest as many, including moral and political theorists, are inclined to suppose. Indeed, as I try to show in chapter 2, a self-interested biological explanation for having children runs afoul. Kantians want to show that morality should have a hold upon our lives regardless of the circumstances in which we find ourselves. Rousseau, if I understand him correctly, saw as clearly as anyone that the kind of moral environment in which we live bears mightily upon the extent to which morality can obtain a secure purchase upon our lives.

The ideas for this book began germinating in 1997 when I gave the Kovler Lectures at the University of Cape Town South Africa. A subsequent trip as a visiting professor gave greater shape to my ideas. I got to witness, first hand, the evil of Apartheid bow to the majesty of goodwill, as people of all backgrounds found it more fruitful to cooperate with one another than to blame one another.[1] Both visits were arranged by the Benatar family, to whom I am so grateful for their friendship and generosity.

The fundamental argument of chapter 1 coalesced as I reflected on the central idea advocated by Dr. Laura C. Schlessinger that children should be our first priority. Although I am well aware that (as a radio talk show host) she is a controversial figure in many respects, it has always seemed to me that the various controversies that swirled around her did not touch the point that children should be the first priority of parents. I have understood her to hold that children are not trophies to be showcased, but gems to be treasured and rendered more radiant. That idea has never ceased to resonate mightily with me. There is no greater love than that which parents have for their children. There is no greater moral gift than parental love. Thus, I concur with Schlessinger that society is as it should be only insofar as it never loses sight of this truth. In listening to her counsel callers, time and time again, not to compare their children with one another, but to affirm the uniqueness of each, I came up

---

[1] Aside from this book, two essays were inspired: "Forgiving the Unforgivable," in Eve Garrard and Geoffrey Scarre (eds.) *Moral Philosophy and the Holocaust* (Burlington, VT: Ashgate Press, 2003), and "Upside-Down Equality: A Response to Kantian Thought" in Michael P. Levine and Tamas Pataki (eds.), *Racism in Mind* (Ithaca, NY: Cornell University Press, 2004).

with the articulation that parental love provides each child with a sense of cherished uniqueness without invidious comparison. I am very grateful to Schlessinger for her encouragement and correspondence with me regarding this matter.

By the time drafts of this book were well underway, Edward McClennen joined the philosophy faculty at Syracuse University. His seminar in social theory was crucial in helping me to formulate the argument that neither parental love nor fellow-feeling is a zero-sum good. He claimed that *I* am one of the reasons he joined the Syracuse University faculty. Perhaps. But while I can readily indicate what I have learned from him, I cannot begin to fathom what he has learned from me. My colleague Michael Stocker served, as he has done throughout my career, as an ever-present sounding board for my inchoate ideas. I am grateful to him for taking my work seriously over the years. He has been a pillar of my professional career.

Joan and Norman Poltenson, of Young Israel Shaari-Torah, have provided me not only with intellectual support, but with the spiritual support of family and community without which life has so much less meaning.

Many parts of this work were written in Paris; and in this regard, I have an enormous debt of gratitude on two accounts. One is to my good friends at the café La Fontaine Saint Michel: the husband and wife team, Carole and Pascal, along with their working partner, Didier. Whenever I would show up, they all marvelously accommodated me, my computer, and my various bits of paper, as I struggled to give form to my ideas. Likewise for the two waiters, Johann and Jean-Paul. Although no one knew much about what I was writing, save what I told them, they all took enormous pride in helping me to complete the project. Indeed, they very warmly referred to me as *their* American, an honor I accept with pride. Without the goodwill of the folks at La Fontaine Saint Michel it would have been impossible to finish this book. My gratitude to them knows no bounds. A l'équipe de La Fontaine Saint Michel, et surtout Carole, Pascal, et Didier: Je vous serai toujours reconnaissant d'avoir été là pour moi.

I should also like to thank the Rougemont family, which ranges over three generations. They have all been a part of my life for so very many years that I cannot imagine Paris without them. Their lives are a marvelous testimony to the richness of the family, and the moral powers that it can occasion. It is rather clear to me that my reading of Rousseau on the family owes much of its inspiration to the Rougemont family. Indeed, when I watch the son Laurent interacting with his two infants, it is almost as if Rousseau wrote about the love of a father for his children with Laurent in mind. That, of course, is a silly thought, since Laurent's very existence was quite some ways off. But I am confident that this silly thought is one that Laurent's wife cherishes. À la famille Rougement: Vous êtes un cadeau du ciel.

Monique Canto-Sperber, Jean-Pierre Dupuy, Bertrand Guillarme, and Ruwen Ogien have all been a wonderful part of my intellectual life in Paris.

A number of people have read various parts of this manuscript: Neera Badwar, David DeGrazia, Howard McGary, Terrence McConnell, Michele Moody-Adams, James Sterba, and Clark Wolf. I am very grateful to them for doing so. It is also the case that Philip Quinn did as well. And it is very painful to me that owing to his untimely death, I cannot express my gratitude to him for doing so.

Finally, I would like to thank several students (past and present) who worked with me on this project: First among these is Nazri Abdel-Aziz, now an instructor in mathematics for SUNY's

College of Environment, Science, and Forestry. The idea of parental loving bestowing a sense of uniqueness without invidious comparison owes much to conversations with him. Nate Federman and Daniel Hoff each read and commented extensively on the first chapter, and helped me to give better articulation to many of my thoughts. Brian Landau has been a model – a veritable Platonic instantiation – of the ideal of gratitude that I have sought to articulate. The same holds for Rawan Jabaji. Furthermore, her wonderful work on friendship inspired me to think of the idea of parental love and fellow-feeling as non-zero-sum goods. As I worked through the edited manuscript, Michael Montgomery proved to be a bundle of energy and inspiration as I wrestled with last-minute formulations. He was invaluable. Michael McFall and Adam Schechter (both graduate students) have been an ever-present sounding board for my thoughts. Their constant presence has been a godsend.

It was Douglas MacLean who was first inclined to think that I had something to say; and it was Norrie Feinblatt who, in her role as copy editor, helped me to say it better.

For Rousseau, the moral sentiments should have center stage in our political reality. Gratitude, I argue, is one of these sentiments. The fortunate life that I have been able to live would never have been possible without the affection and goodwill of so many people. Thank you.

Syracuse, NY
February 2005

Introduction

Having children is one of the most common projects among adult human beings throughout history and across differences among human beings. The aim of having children transcends differences in religious traditions, as well as racial differences and a variety of physical differences. Adults with physical impairments are no less desirous of children than those without such impairments. What is more, having children transcends the widest possible economic and educational disparities, including even dramatic differences in freedom. Thus, even under the burden of slavery, during which many black females were forcibly impregnated, it is true nonetheless that many blacks chose to have children.

In many cases, adults want and seek to have children whatever else they do as adults and regardless of whatever other successes they may have as adults. To this end, in fact, adults will often go to extraordinary means, spending large sums of money and subjecting themselves to grueling procedures. In vitro fertilization, for instance, comes readily to mind. And I shall leave aside entirely the issue of cloning that looms large on the horizon. In any case, children are often thought to give both a completion and a meaning to life that nothing else can give. While we certainly think that a person can have a remarkably meaningful life without children, there is at least the tendency to think that children (can) contribute to a meaningful and complete life in a way that nothing else (can) does. Surely professional success, fame, and fortune are not thought to render children otiose. On the contrary, many who enjoy these aspects of life often seek to complete their lives by having children, where raising and being involved in the lives of one's children are thought to provide an incomparable richness to life that cannot be had otherwise.

To be sure, there can be good reasons, such as health, for not having children. Still, wanting to have children is not a want that anyone generally has to explain. Far from it. What often seems to mystify and require an explanation is a person's not wanting to have any children at all. Not only that, the more well-off we think a person is in terms of having the resources to make for a good parent, the more it seems to us that having children is the reasonable thing for the person to do. In fact, folk wisdom often characterizes a person who refrains from having children as selfish. Interestingly in this regard, the one explanation for not having children that seems to be the most palatable from the outset is the pursuit of a religious calling. And here it is not so much that the existence of the want is denied; rather, the want is thought to be sublimated to what is considered a higher calling. Moreover, the pursuit of a religious calling is typically characterized by folk wisdom as an altruistic endeavor; hence, this pursuit rebuts the charge of selfishness. If being a rational animal capable of self-locomotion is a defining feature of the essence of a human being, then having children would seem to be one of the defining features of the practical life of a human being.

The above is, of course, a very bold and broad characterization regarding one of the central aims of human beings. I have spoken of the aim of having children in a rather noble way. Yet, it is manifestly clear that people often have children for reasons that are far from noble. For some, having children is rather like acquiring a marvelous trophy that they can now showcase and brag about. The hired nanny knows more about the child than the parents.[1] For others, if talk shows are to be believed, having children is a way of getting even or proving one's adulthood. Just so, even after one has allowed for the ignoble reasons for which people have children; and even after one has allowed for the fact that some people do not want the children that they bring into this world and bring home; and even after one has allowed for the reality that more people nowadays are quite self-consciously choosing not to have children: the claim that in general people want to have children stands as true as the claim that in general people want to have more rather than less money. No one thinks that this claim about money is vitiated by fact that some people with considerable ability choose careers that pay less well than other careers, and that others still go so far as to take vows of poverty. In a like manner, the claim is not that every single person wants to have a child. That is manifestly false. Rather, what is being advanced is the more modest, but yet quite significant, claim that having children is one of the most common human activities that transcends all human categories. It is what most people want to do, and in fact do, whatever else they might choose to do.

One might question the validity of folk wisdom on the grounds that a proper account of the project of having children, indeed, admits of a self-interested interpretation rather than an altruistic one. Evolutionary theory is generally invoked here. I shall show in chapter 2 that evolutionary theory does not at all require a self-interested interpretation of human beings having children. Furthermore, I shall show that the sense in which political theory

---

[1] For a very provocative book in this regard, see Laura C. Schlessinger, *Parenting by Proxy* (New York: Harper Collins, 2000).

claims that persons are self-interested does not apply to having children.

Before continuing, three brief points of clarification are in order. The first is this. The expression "having a child" is, strictly speaking, ambiguous between, on the one hand, simply bearing a child and, on the other, bearing a child and raising it. A woman may bear a child and not raise it. She may put it up for adoption or, painfully, the child might not live. The overwhelming majority of women wish to raise the children whom they bear. Alternatively, owing to adoption, it is possible to raise a child without bearing any children whatsoever. Significantly, most people want to bear the children whom they raise; and adoption at infancy, which is the preferred mode of adoption, is intended to get as close as is humanly possible to raising a child from birth without actually birthing the child. Hence, the fees for adopting a newborn infant are much higher than are the fees for adopting, say, a three-year-old child. In any event, there is no reason whatsoever to think that in order to achieve the aim of raising children, adoption would ever become preferable to birthing children. If it did, however, this would not threaten the impulse of my argument, as we shall see. People want to raise children whom they regard as their own. Birth unequivocally achieves this end; adoption at infancy is the next closest thing. What is more, the significance of having children lies not so much in giving birth to them – which is hardly trivial, to be sure – but in raising them. Although I shall use the language of "having children," it should be understood to cover adoption as well. This should also be understood to cover raising children. This is how we normally speak. When a person claims to want to have a child, we typically understand that the person wants both to bear a child and to raise the child that she bears, unless the individual immediately sets the record straight. There are exceptions, of course, such as serving as a surrogate womb for another. These do not count against the force of the argument.

The second point of clarification pertains to bearing children and the sex act. Although bearing children naturally, if that is the word for it, is a probable consequence of the sex act (between fertile individuals of the opposite sex), it is obvious that people may want to engage in the sex act without wanting to conceive a child. However, I did not make the ridiculous claim that people want to conceive a child every time they engage in the sex act. Rather, I have claimed that wanting children is a common desire that transcends all differences. This claim is compatible with people having more children than they wanted to have or having a child at a time when they did not want to have one.

Third, although it is perhaps true that a great many people want to have more than one child, this is not the thesis of this book. In claiming that having children is the most common of all human projects, I mean only to be making the very weak claim that most people want to have at least one child.

Now, if it is obvious that having children is such a common project among human beings, it is profoundly striking that this most human of all human projects does not have center place among political theory construction. Typically, political theories concern themselves with how adults interact with other adults. On the one hand, there is the issue of adults bargaining with one another in order for each to get what she or he wants. On the other, there is the issue of each adult curtailing her or his aims in order to show the proper amount of respect for another adult. The problem with this two-prong model is that it dramatically fails to capture the project of having a child. For the very essence of the project of having children is not that of either bargaining with another adult in order to obtain something or refraining from doing something in the name of respecting another adult, but that of bringing life into this world or nurturing life from its infancy (as with infant adoption). More specifically, the project of having children is about voluntarily choosing to take on a significant moral responsibility for a new life. What is more, this is an end in itself. Having children is not just one among any other project that a person might wish to realize. Quite the contrary, the very nature of the project is understandably thought to be fundamentally different, because bringing a life into the world and raising it is, indeed, quite unlike any other project that a person might pursue. What is more, the fact that people expend great sums of money in order either to conceive a child or to adopt one, and thus to have this enormous responsibility of caring for a life, indicates that parenting is a task unlike any other in terms of its significance in the lives of individuals. It is one thing to take on great responsibility; it is quite another to make great sacrifices in order to do so, where there is no public honor or public prestige that comes with doing so as with politics. Nor is there any form of substantial remuneration save the delight that one takes in caring for the object of one's responsibility. Furthermore, the eagerness – and that is precisely the word for it – of people to adopt when all else fails underscores even more dramatically the significance that individuals place on raising a child.

Much of political theory takes it as a given that human beings are essentially self-interested or that for all practical purposes we might as well think of them that way. But this way of viewing human beings is rather at odds with the idea that having children is one of the most central projects that human beings take themselves to have. For, as I shall show in chapter 2, the project of having children does not lend itself to a self-interested interpretation, at least not as this idea has been traditionally understood. Indeed, as I have already noted, folklore has it that those who do not have children are self-interested, unless, of course, they are answering to a higher calling.

The line of thought here in folklore is straightforward enough. No matter how much delight parents take in raising their children, parenting requires making significant sacrifices from time to time for the sake of their children; hence, parenting requires a measure of altruism. There is absolutely no way to be a decent parent and opt out of making such sacrifices from time to time. While monetary sacrifices may come readily to mind, this is hardly the only sacrifice that parents may have to make on behalf of their children. For instance, well-off parents may have to forgo an extraordinary career opportunity or business adventure. By contrast, the person who refrains from having children – not owing to religious reasons – is one who thereby chooses not to do that which would require her or him to sometimes make sacrifices for another. Although a person without children may take on other altruistic endeavors, such as becoming a Big Brother or a Big Sister, the individual is free to opt out of them. Relocating for career considerations is, for instance, a perfectly good reason to bring a Big Brother or Big Sister relationship in the original city to a close. This occasions a loss on the child's part that no one denies, but that everyone understands. Indeed, simply the pursuit of a romantic interest in another city many hundreds of miles away suffices as a good reason to opt out; whereas no single parent can rightly opt out of parental requirements in pursuit of a romantic interest. These considerations alone are certainly consistent with folk wisdom that parenting is altruistic in a way that non-parenting as such is not. To be sure, this does not make the nonparent without a religious vocation selfish. Just so, one can see the line of thought that gives rise to the presumption that parenting is altruistic.

Now given the importance and the altruistic nature of parenting, it is quite ironic that political theory assumes that most people are self-interested without ever addressing the fact that most people have children and that, in doing so, most people do what is commonly held to be contrary to the idea of relentlessly promoting their self-interest.[2] Traditionally, self-interest is to be understood in terms of a baseline. An act is in (*contrary to*) a person's self-interest if it raises (*lowers*) the individual above (*below*) that baseline. To be sure, much refinement is possible here, since from the outset what counts as the baseline can be a matter of great dispute and, moreover, the baseline can change over time. Thus, whereas having a high school diploma was once upon a time the baseline for getting a decent job, it is arguable that the baseline is now a bachelor's degree. Similarly, the baseline for poverty changes, because it corresponds to the level of economic prosperity in a society. At any rate, one thing is clear: the notion of self-interest will have become more than a little eviscerated if with far fewer resources left, or notwithstanding great

---

[2] In understanding the role of self-interest in moral and political philosophy, my first intellectual debt is to Kurt Baier, *The Moral Point of View* (Ithaca, NY: Cornell University Press, 1958), and then to David Gauthier, *Morals by Agreement* (New York: Oxford University Press, 1986). Intellectual heir to Baier, Gauthier is perhaps the first contemporary theorist to make the assumption of self-interest so explicitly and unapologetically in his work, and yet with the hope of establishing an altruistic conception of morality. Neither, however, addresses the fact that having children seems to be the central project of most adults in the world, whatever else their aims are. So neither addresses the fact that, in having children, people commonly do what is held in some way not to be in their self-interest. I have discussed Gauthier's self-interested project in "Rationality and Affectivity: The Metaphysics of the Moral Self," *Social Philosophy and Policy* 5 (1988): 154–72. However, I must acknowledge that I, too, did not think to invoke the project of having children. My inspiration for the present text owes much to the work of Roger D. Masters's remarkable essay "Evolutionary Biology and Political Theory," *American Political Science Review* 84 (1990).

opportunities that were forgone, a person can still say that her or his self-interest has been maximized. Yet, people often say that they are better off on account of having children although they acknowledge that they are worse off because they now have fewer resources than when they started out or that they forwent a few marvelous opportunities. And one very strong evidence of sincerity here is that people rarely regret having children, notwithstanding the costs involved. To be sure, our view of children has changed somewhat; and I shall say something about this momentarily. Still, if having children is one of the most common human projects and, moreover, this project does not readily admit of a self-interested interpretation, then something is amiss if political theory ignores these two stark truths. If throughout history, and across every conceivable set of circumstances, the overwhelming majority of people who take vows of poverty were to turn out to be those with red hair, one would expect political theory to reflect this reality.

This book, then, is meant as a corrective to political theory in contemporary thought. The basic idea at least in the tradition of social contract theory is that under conditions of scarcity it is in the best interest of adult human beings, understood as essentially self-interested, to cooperate. Then the trick is to get a stable commitment to an altruistic morality or conception of justice from this simple truth. To this end, tremendous intellectual ingenuity has been pressed into service, from the metaphysics of taking oneself seriously over time to considerations of long-term self-interests, to the nature and force of promising or keeping an agreement. Somehow, some way, it is supposed to turn out that in the end self-interest no longer has anything like the dramatic pull that it was alleged to have at the outset. Self-interest is supposed to cease to be the very fount of motivation. In response to exactly how this extraordinary feat is supposed to happen there seems to be an awful lot of what I would call disingenuous *amicus ad hominem*: "If you cannot see how the argument works (or certainly would work with just few a extra innocuous assumptions), then may I politely suggest that you do not properly understand it."

Well, as I have noted, whatever else people decide to do, they generally have children. Moreover, they voluntarily choose to do this. And this simple fact would suggest that the initial characterization of adult human beings as essentially self-interested stands in need of correction. My aim in this book is to bring out how significant a difference this simple fact makes in how we understand ourselves as human beings.

Although much of the history of political theory has attached very little importance to the fact that adults have children, there are two shining exceptions, namely Plato and, centuries later, Rousseau who was a great admirer of Plato.[3] There is no plausible reading of the *Republic* whereby Plato's construction of the state can be understood in terms of adults trying to get the most for themselves. And Rousseau makes the following tantalizing claim:

> The family is the first model of political societies. The head of society corresponds to the position of the father; whereas the people, themselves, correspond to the image of the children. What is more, all are born equal. . . . The only difference is that with the family, the love of the father for his children is what, as it were, rewards him for that which he does on their behalf.   (*Emile* Bk I, Ch. 1)

Since we typically presume that there is a natural affinity between family members rather than some natural enmity to be overcome,

---

3 Rousseau wrote: "If one wishes to have a really excellent idea of a fundamentally just society, one must read Plato's *Republic*. This is not just a political work, as is often supposed by those who judge books solely by their titles, this is the most beautiful treatise on education ever developed." *Emile*, Book I.

then by extension it would seem that Rousseau held that there is a natural affinity between the members of society. Hence, taming self-interest is not the fundamental building block of civil society. Indeed, regarding the move from the State of Nature to Civil Society, Rousseau writes:

> Whatever advantages man is deprived of in the State of Nature, he fully regains in Civil Society. His faculties are engaged and fully developed, his ideas are broadened, his sentiments are ennobled. Indeed, his very soul is completely elevated.
>
> Man should continuously bless that wonderful moment when he was uprooted forever from the state of being a stupid and limited animal in the State of Nature, and made an intelligent being and a man in Civil Society.

This page reads as if something other than a taming of self-interest takes place in the move from the State of Nature to Civil Society; and I shall take up this matter in chapter 4.

Just so, my aim in this book is not to defend the thought of either Plato or Rousseau. Perhaps their views are ultimately indefensible because of their conception of women. Nonetheless, I am very much inspired by the thought advanced by both concerning the importance of attending to children even if their thought was executed in unacceptable ways. My own view is that it is only when we take seriously the role of having children in the lives of adults that we can see how much contributing to the flourishing of another is such a fundamental feature of what it is to be a human being. The book has two parts. In part 1, Life's Beginning, I offer an account of what it means, morally speaking, to take seriously the project of having a child. In part 2, The Crucible of Society, I argue that who we are as adults is inextricably tied to the fact that we can take seriously the project of having, or in any case raising, children.

As I have already indicated, I am mindful of the fact that not all adults have children, and that others still choose, for various reasons, to adopt children. It is a fundamentally important datum that people who adopt children can show them all the love that any biological parent could possibly show. This makes it unmistakably clear that among human beings parental love is not conceptually tied to a biological connection between the parents and the child.

I am also mindful of the fact that the view that we have of children today has changed dramatically over the years. In John Locke's writings, children are very nearly viewed as nothing other than a form of property. This is hardly surprising, given his emphasis upon owning that with which one mixed one's labor to achieve. After all, if children are not a result of the mixing of labor in some sense between two people, then surely nothing is! Today, however, many societies give children an independent importance that was very nearly unthinkable even in the early part of the twentieth century, let alone hundreds of years ago. The stories of young adolescents and pre-teenage children working in mines and factories nine or ten decades ago leave us utterly aghast,[4] to say nothing of the sexual exploitation of children. In times past, sexual relations with a child, even when frowned upon, were seen at best as nothing more than a minor temporary inconvenience to the child rather than something that left an indelible psychological scar.[5] Today, we have a much more

---

[4] See the riveting photographs by Lewis W. Hines in Russell Freedman, *Kids at Work: Lewis Hines and the Crusade Against Child Labor* (Clarion Books, 1998). For an excellent account of the early history of child labor, see Edith Abott, "A Study of the Early History of Child Labor in America," *American Journal of Sociology* 14 (1908).

[5] For a most intriguing discussion of this, see Ian Hacking, *Rewriting the Soul: Multiple Personality and the Sciences of Memory* (Princeton: Princeton University Press, 1995), ch. 2.

informed view of the fragility of the child and the circumstances necessary for its developing in a wholesome way. It is, quite simply, utterly inappropriate for parents to see their child as but a mere extension of their will. What is striking is that the desire to have children has remained quite constant, even though a means-end conception of children has lost its hold upon people's thinking. In the move from agrarian societies (where children were presumed to be useful for farming) to highly industrialized societies (where children did not have a like utility), the desire to have children has not dropped precipitously. What has changed, rather, is that people are having fewer children. In fact, many couples are very deliberately choosing to have only one child; and this choice alone, if it becomes a sufficiently widespread pattern, suffices to yield a decline in the birth rate. Needless to say, though, what is of the utmost significance for the purposes of this book is just the fact that the vast majority of couples still very much want to have at least one child.

Undoubtedly, our attitude toward having children has been influenced by, among other things, the control that we now have over our reproductive organs. With considerable mastery, we have de-coupled conception from the sex act, thus acquiring enormous control over whether, and in particular when, we have children. Once more, though, none of this has in any substantial way abated the desire among peoples across the world, and across a multitude of differences, to have children. People are still having children. On the assumption that nothing more profoundly reveals our desires than what we choose to do when we could just as easily do otherwise, the fact that adult humans are very likely to embark on the project of having (or raising) children, whatever else they do as adults, is a most significant consideration that should not be overlooked. Sterilization techniques are readily available. Yet, people rarely avail themselves of such techniques before embarking on a sexual life (as if they had not a clue that there might be a connection between sex and conception). Is it that with regard to having children people are that obtuse or thoughtless? Perhaps. The more plausible explanation, though, is that people want to be open to the possibility of the transmission of life, and sterilization forecloses that option.

A final introductory remark. As we know, life is often very messy. I have already noted that people have children for a variety of reasons, not all of which are even remotely noble. These ignoble considerations notwithstanding, a fundamental assumption of this book is not that every child is conceived because its parents wanted to bring into this world a life that they can love. We know that this is definitely not the case. Whether every child is wanted at the outset or not, it is true nonetheless that parents can adopt the *wanted-out-of-love stance* toward each and every child,[6] if they so choose. No child, however conceived, need be told by its parents that it was unwanted. After all, it cannot possibly be thought that love can be genuine only if persons have voluntarily sought to have ties with those whom they love. For this would undermine the very idea of children loving their parents, since it cannot in any way be said that a child chooses either to be born or to have the parents that the infant has. People do not always love the children whom they conceive, even when the conception was intentional. But the capacity for human excellence is not shown to be nonexistent simply because it is

---

[6] Obviously, the wording here owes its inspiration to Daniel C. Dennett, *Content and Consciousness* (London: Routledge & Kegan Paul, 1969), and what he calls the intentional stance. Just as obviously, however, I am not embracing Dennett's conception of the self.

not always displayed among human beings. The impetus for this book is the moral excellence of which human beings are capable – not the moral squalor that so often characterizes the human condition.

I have just remarked that no child, however conceived, need ever be told that it was unwanted, because adopting the wanted-out-of-love stance is always an option. With every option, including the option to go on living itself, the exercise of that option is easier for some than others. It would be foolish to deny that it is easier for some people to adopt the wanted-out-of-love stance than it is for others. Nor, perhaps, should we deny that it is easier in particular for women to adopt this stance, since the child comes out of their bodies after nine months.

That said, I most certainly do not mean to discount the travails and evils of sexism in the absence of reproductive control.[7] In so many ways, though, this speaks to the point regarding the wherewithal to adopt the wanted-out-of-love stance. Were it not for the truth that in the midst of sexist oppression women could adopt the wanted-out-of-love stance, many a child born under circumstances of sexist oppression would have gone unloved. Significantly, evil invariably highlights the excellence of which human beings are capable. Sexist oppression is wrong; yet it reveals something about the moral capacity of human beings, namely the wherewithal to adopt the wanted-out-of-love stance.

---

[7] Indeed, in 1980 I went against the grain in arguing that sexism is deeper than racism, because gender identity is the more fundamental form of identity. See my "Sexism and Racism: Some Conceptual Differences," *Ethics* 90 (1980). The depth of gender identity can also explain increasingly less sexist behavior in males. It is better to evolve socially as a man if the result is that one is more likely to be seen as desirable by women. A like interplay does not hold between ethnic identities.

Women can adopt this stance and so can men. For to say that a task is easier, if indeed it is easier for women, is not thereby to excuse a person from performing it. In the case at hand, this may simply mean that men must take extra steps to ensure that they do their part. The wherewithal to adopt the wanted-out-of-love stance is among one of our most extraordinary human excellences.[8]

---

[8] In several important essays, David Benatar defends with great ingenuity the view that being born is not, in and of itself, the benefit that it is typically made out to be. I should note that strictly speaking the views advanced in this book are compatible with his claim. On the one hand, the theses that people are generally eager to have children and that parental love is majestic do not, either individually or jointly, entail that we are all better off on account of having been born. On the other, Benatar's view is certainly compatible with the view that parental love is of enormous importance, given that one has been brought into existence. These essays are: "Why it is Better Never to Come into Existence," *American Philosophical Quarterly* 34 (1997); "The Wrong of Wrongful Life," *American Philosophical Quarterly* 37 (2000); "To Be or Not to Have Been?: Defective Counterfactual Reasoning About One's Own Existence," *International Journal of Applied Philosophy* 15 (2001). Hugh Lafollette, in "Licensing Parents," *Philosophy and Public Affairs* 9 (1980), has argued that there should be criteria for ruling out truly objectionable parents. Philip Montague, in "The Myth of Parental Rights," *Social Theory and Practice* 26 (2000), defends the even stronger view that biological parents do not have rights over their children. I concur with the substance of Montague's view, which is essentially that a child should be raised by individuals who will properly care for her or him and that being a child's biological parents is no guarantee that the child will be raised in this way. When biological parents should be allowed to raise their children is a most important issue that I do not address in this book.

PART I

LIFE'S BEGINNING

1

Uniquely Valued

A child who was treated morally, but who went unloved, is a child who would not, and could not, come to value itself properly. Nothing more fully bestows a sense of worth upon a newborn child than parental love. As infants, we are born into this world without a sense of self and so without a sense of value. And it is parental love, and nothing else, that at the outset makes it possible for us to have a proper sense of self. Anything else will invariably miss the mark. It is by virtue of being the unmistakable object of manifest parental love that we come to have a positive sense of worth, that we come to value ourselves as human beings. Indeed, in the absence of parental love, no sense of worth could easily obtain a purchase upon our lives, including moral worth. Thus, while there is no denying that morality is an intrinsic good, it is not first among intrinsic goods. *Parental love is.* From the standpoint of the development of our soul, parental love is more basic than morality.

1 CHERISHED UNIQUENESS

What explains this difference between parental love and morality? The answer is poignant by virtue of its simplicity. Of course, a moral person is one who treats others in the right way. All the same, a moral person may be indifferent to whether or not, in the first place, others come into being. There is no antecedent desire or longing for their existence. Indeed, a moral person who devotes her entire life to helping others need not have wanted any of those whom she helped to have come into existence; though, to be sure, she will not bemoan their existence. What is more, a person can be quite morally upright without taking it upon herself to promote the flourishing of others. The moral person has an abiding commitment not to wrong others. However, one can have this commitment without taking a substantial interest in promoting the well-being of others.

By contrast, the simple but ever so powerful presumption that comes in the wake of parental love is that the child's very existence was, and continues to be, wanted. Thus, it is not just the fact that a child is loved. There is the absolutely extraordinary consideration that *the child was brought into being in order to be loved*. Moreover, there is not just an acceptance of the child's flourishing, but a commitment to this taking place. Accordingly, a child's sense of worth is properly underwritten when, and only when, the child experiences the behavior of its parents on its behalf as an immutable commitment to its well-being that they did not have to have, but chose to have. It is precisely this delight that parents take in their child's existence (both its coming into being and its being) that simply has no counterpart in morality. Thus, it is parental love and only parental love that generates in the child what I shall call a sense of *cherished uniqueness not tied to invidious comparisons*.[1] When things go as they should, the child's

---

[1] In his important essay "Love as a Moral Emotion," *Ethics* 109 (1999), J. David Velleman asks: "How valuable can our uniqueness make us if everyone is unique?" (p. 363). On the account being offered here, I think that Velleman's challenge

conviction that she is profoundly loved by her parents does not in any way require the belief on the part of the child that she is more loved by her parents than other children are loved by their parents. Nor does parental love engender the sentiment that the child is better than other children. Parental love does not engender these sentiments notwithstanding the fact that parents privilege their children and not the children of others. Thus, the very nature of parental love is that it privileges without entailing invidious comparisons. Morality, by contrast, does not privilege. I shall say a word about that momentarily.

can be met. For parents can say to their children that the children's uniqueness lies in the parents' bringing them into this world in order to love them. Velleman's very fascinating concern is that the ubiquity of uniqueness is self-defeating with regard to uniqueness. Interestingly, parental love is less threatened by this problem, if at all, than romantic love. This is because parental love is tied to the relation "being the parent/child of." No other child ever gets to be the child of a different set of parents, the special case of adoption aside. So there really is an irreplaceability that is operative. With romantic love, the problem is that people can be replaced. Indeed, they often are. Of course, the experiences that one has with a given lover will be *sui generis*. However, there is no transcendent relation analogous to "being the parent/child of" that operates between lovers that provides an independent guarantee to uniqueness. I believe that Velleman's challenge underscores the importance of parental love, as well as the importance of moral theory taking seriously this aspect of life.

The idea of cherished uniqueness not tied to invidious comparisons was inspired by the work of Francis Schrag. See, e.g., his essays "Justice and the Family," *Inquiry* 19 (1976) and "The Child and the Moral Order," *Philosophy* 52 (1977), and "The Child's Status in the Democratic State," *Political Theory* 3 (1975). In the third essay, Schrag forcefully raises the issue of intellectual competence. I hold that the defining difference between an adult and a child has nothing whatsoever to do with differences in intellectual competence per se, but with the raw psychological need that children have to be valued. Hence, the idea of being uniquely cherished without invidious comparisons. Relevant here is the account of parental love as transparent that I offered in *Living Morally: A Psychology of Moral Character* (Philadelphia, PA: Temple University Press, 1989), chapter 2.

Needless to say, to have a sense of cherished uniqueness is also to have a sense of intrinsic worth. For cherished uniqueness, as I am understanding it, is not at all something that one can earn. The child who is brought into this world to be loved cannot possibly be thought to have earned that standing with her or his parents. Not surprisingly, I want to say that the intrinsic worth that comes with parental love is more basic.

Significantly, nature provides all that is needed in order for parents to engender in their children a sense of cherished uniqueness without invidious comparisons. Of course, the appropriate resolve on the part of parents is necessary. However, being effective in displaying parental love is not in any way tied to a person's economic or social standing or educational level. Under the poorest of conditions, a child can justifiably feel ever so loved by her parents; under the wealthiest of conditions, a child can justifiably feel ever so unloved and neglected by his parents. It is an indisputable truth that no amount of material goods, however marvelous, can substitute for the simple expressions of love by a parent. With regard to education, we know that highly educated parents may ignore their child, because the child is just one among many projects which compete for the time that the parents have; whereas parents with a very humble education may dote mightily on their child. Regardless of how they are socially situated, all parents can convey to their child the idea that she or he was brought into this world to be loved by them without in any way indicating to the child that she or he is superior to other children. With regard to providing parental love, and so engendering a sense of cherished uniqueness, nature did not favor the wealthy or the beautiful or the well-educated.

As an aside, the preceding remarks might shed some light on the universal appeal of becoming a parent. For parenting allows for the very real hope of doing something morally majestic whatever one's station in life might be, just so long as the bond between parent and child remains stable and wholesome. The poor or uneducated person can have this hope as much as the wealthy or the scholarly. It is a sublime feature of our humanity that with respect to the extraordinary act of parenting human beings are so very equal from the standpoint of nature.

At any rate, parental love at its best achieves what morality cannot. Perhaps even more sublimely stated, it is by virtue of parental love that the child experiences being treated morally not as a duty, but as an act of love. Although every loving parent is deeply motivated to treat her or his child in all the morally right ways, the springs of that motivation are most surely not morality itself. It is surely not for the sake of duty, to use Kant's own language, that good parents do what is right by their children. Thus, parental love challenges Kantian morality in a very deep way. For there is at least one category of the person, namely that of a child, who should be treated morally where the ultimate motivational basis for such treatment should not be morality, but love itself. That Kantian moral theory misses this point is striking; and this further underscores the claim that children are roundly ignored in moral and political theory construction. Why? Because Kantian theory does not have self-interested moorings. Rather, it has a very rich and subtle metaphysics of the moral self that is far removed from self-interest. Yet, for all of Kantian theory's distance from self-interest, it turns out that the most selfless of human activities in which persons deliberately and routinely engage, namely having children, is not aptly captured.

When it comes to saving a person's life or not stealing, for instance, it is at least arguable that acting from the motive of duty, as Kant and Kantians would say, is superior to acting from love.

This is certainly so when it comes to strangers. And in some cases, overcoming desire in order to do one's duty is, indeed, most admirable. All the same, when it comes to parenting there is simply no way in which doing the right thing from the motive of duty can on a general basis be judged superior to doing the right thing from the motive of love, whatever the behavior in question might be. Not even parental punishment is the exception here. Whereas love, as such, is irrelevant to morality, love is a quintessential aspect of parenting. One can have morality at its best without love. Not so with parenting. Interestingly, the debate with regard to motives between Kantians and virtue ethicists has been cast in terms of interactions between adult friends rather than between parent and child. This difference here is far from trivial because even if it is arguable that friends do what is right in helping one another when they are motivated by duty rather than by love, it is just implausible to argue this in terms of parenting. While friends have the psychological wherewithal to accept the Kantian line of thought, if only begrudgingly, it is manifestly false that children do.[2] To state the obvious: Adult-adult interactions are not the same as adult-child interactions; and any moral theory that ignores this misses the mark in a fundamental way.

I have already noted that one fundamental difference between the love of parenting and morality is that at its best the former embodies the ideal that the child is wanted so that it may be loved, whereas this is not so with morality. But it is also important to see

---

[2] Cf. Lawrence Blum, *Friendship, Altruism, and Morality* (Boston: Routlege Press, 1980), for one of the central critics of Kant's thought in the debate regarding love, motives, and moral duty. See also, Michael Stocker, "The Schizophrenia of Modern Ethical Theory" *Journal of Philosophy* 73 (1976); and Bernard Williams, "Persons, Character, and Morality" in his *Moral Luck* (New York: Cambridge University Press, 1981).

that the very structure of morality is at odds with bestowing upon individuals a sense of cherished uniqueness without invidious comparison.

Morality, by its very nature, is not person-specific. Everyone should be treated properly, not just tall people or people who do not need to wear eyeglasses or wealthy people; not just so-and-so next door or up the street or across town. Morality is about how anyone and everyone should be treated in the relevant circumstances. Accordingly, if a given feature makes a difference for one person, then morality requires that this very same feature make a difference for all other persons similarly situated. For example, if being near death owing to starvation morally excuses Rachel's act of stealing a bit of food in order to stay alive, then this consideration morally excuses everyone so situated from so behaving. Indeed, morality cannot privilege a person as such, but only the particularities of a person's circumstances. Thus, insofar as Rachel is justified in stealing, this has nothing whatsoever to do with the fact that she is Rachel, but with the fact that she is near death from starvation.

Recall Thomas Nagel's remarkable book, *The Possibility of Altruism.*[3] He reminds us that according to the moral point of view, each person counts for no more than one among others. The egoist, Nagel observes, wants to count for more than one among others. That is, she wants to hold that her concerns are more important than the concerns of others because and only because the concerns are hers. Nagel argues that such a person is guilty of conceptual confusion and cannot have any rational grounds for thinking this. Each person counts, but no more than any other person. Hence, as a purely structural matter cherished

---

[3] (New York: Oxford University Press, 1970).

uniqueness has no place in the moral point of view. Indeed, a conception of morality that embodied the view that cherished uniqueness holds for some individuals would not on Nagel's account be a conception of morality at all.

I claimed at the outset that it is parental love by way of engendering a sense of cherished uniqueness that enables moral worth to obtain a secure footing upon our lives. Let me make good that claim. I shall begin with a thought experiment.

Imagine an excellent reader entirely bereft of a sense of intrinsic moral worth reading the superb arguments that have been presented to show that all persons have intrinsic moral self-worth. There is no shortage of quite good arguments here. Let us suppose, though, that he reads Thomas Hill's classic essay "Servility and Self-Respect,"[4] which he (the reader) finds extremely intuitive and quite persuasive. Our reader sees how the Deferential Housewife and the Uncle Tom whom Hill describes are servile because both of them fail to attach sufficient weight to their own moral value. Moreover, suppose that through these two examples our reader is able to recognize his own failure in this regard. Coming from a home in which he was both sexually and physically abused with regularity, our reader now has a cognitive grasp of the moral flaw that his excessively deferential behavior reveals. Thanks to reading Hill's essay, he understands that he is being not just kind or considerate, but morally servile.

Now, it is tempting to say that it is rather unlikely that someone so bereft of a sense of moral worth is going to change so radically in his thinking about such matters simply in virtue of reading a very good philosophical argument. There would certainly

---

4 Hill's *Servility and Autonomy and Self-Respect* (New York: Cambridge University Press, 1991). The essay originally appeared in *The Monist* 57 (1973).

be a point to this contention. This need not much concern us, though. This is because even if we allow that the person now has different thoughts about the matter of servility and his servility in particular, it would be absolutely stunning if argument alone would bring about genuine change in the person's feelings toward himself. Although the reading may very well bring about the desire on the person's part to have a sense of intrinsic moral worth, it will not bring about that sense of moral worth itself. It is out of the question that a person entirely bereft of a sense of intrinsic moral worth could actually come to have this feeling, in any settled way, merely upon reading Hill's essay or, for that matter, reading any other writing on the subject, including Kant's own work. For it is next to impossible that a prevailing sense of moral inadequacy could be dismantled by a reading alone. This is because a deep sense of intrinsic moral worth and a deep sense of servility are both psychological dispositions; and either the formation or dismantling of psychological dispositions requires time and, moreover, the appropriate experiences in life.[5] Consider the point from the other direction. Although there are lots of people in the world with an adequate sense of

[5] I believe that Kantians discount the extent to which the appropriate experience is relevant to having a sense of intrinsic moral worth. Some of this stems from the fact that for Kant and Kantians, the term "person" is more of a term of art than is realized. I have discussed this in "Moral Equality and Natural Inferiority," *Social Theory and Practice* 31 (2005). My essay is an extensive comment on the very subtle essay "Race and Kant" by Thomas Hill, Jr. and Bernard Boxill in Boxill (ed.) *Race and Racism* (New York: Oxford University Press, 2001). In a masterful essay, "Dignity, Slavery, and the Thirteenth Amendment," in Michael Meyer and William Parent (eds.), *The Constitution of Rights* (Ithaca, NY: Cornell University Press, 1992), Boxill argues that personhood stands as a kind of natural kind for which it makes no sense to ask for proof that one is a person. This I accept. But as people like Kant, Jefferson, and Tocqueville used the expression, not all persons possessed the same capacities; and I argue

worth, we would find utterly incredulous the claim that a person now lacks a sense of worth merely from reading a text in which persons of his background have a low sense of worth.

2 EXPERIENCE AND UNDERWRITING INTRINSIC MORAL WORTH

Persons with a deep sense of intrinsic moral worth are those who value themselves in the morally right way and, moreover, who have the repeated experience of so valuing themselves in contexts where their intrinsic moral worth is contested. Proper self-valuing is, if you will, a habit of character. Their repeated experiences of proper moral self-valuing serve to underwrite their sense of intrinsic moral worth. What is more, and this gets to the very heart of the matter, such individuals feel quite uneasy when their moral self-worth is being called into question. By contrast, things are the other way around with morally servile persons. Their failure to accord themselves sufficient moral value is also a habit of character; and their servile sense of self is thereby underwritten by this pattern of behavior. Quite importantly, being modest is readily confused with the viewpoint that it was appropriate that they were passed over or unacknowledged. The upshot of our simple thought experiment in the preceding section is this: Persons who do not value themselves as having intrinsic moral worth – such as the morally servile – will not come to value themselves simply by being exposed to philosophical arguments that deliver the conclusion that this is so. Rather, they very much need to have the experience of so valuing themselves.

that where the differences in capacities are great enough, then we could in fact have a moral difference.

What is more, when it comes to having a sense of intrinsic moral worth, surely the capacity to understand the requisite philosophical arguments come too late in the day in most cases. That is, we would hope that a person has a sense of worth long before being able to understand the philosophical arguments to this effect. The major moral theories were advanced by extraordinarily gifted individuals; and other very talented individuals have discussed, critiqued, and interpreted these theories. For instance, *A Theory of Justice* by John Rawls is acknowledged to be the most influential moral and political theory of the twentieth century. Yet, Rawls's work is in many respects an ingenious elaboration of Kant's thought. It is just plain foolish to suppose that the typical twenty-year-old, to say nothing of a younger person, could adequately understand even Rawls's theory, to say nothing of Kant's, if only such a youth were to apply himself. Yet, we should hope that the typical twenty-year-old already has a deep sense of intrinsic moral worth or is well on his way to having it. Indeed, many would hold that if a society is just, then such is the case. For we know that things do not bode well for the twenty-year-old who is not already well on her or his way to having a deep sense of intrinsic moral worth.

Now, many things in life allow for well-defined practice exercises before fully participating in the activity in question. There are training schools for running vehicles of public transportation and pilot lessons for flying airplanes. Teachers of elementary schools must first be certified; and a medical doctor can open a private practice only after completing an internship. Not so when it comes to intrinsic moral worth. There are no training schools for having a sense of intrinsic moral worth. There are no formal modes of certification in this regard. That is, having a sense of intrinsic moral worth cannot be made to hang upon the knowledge that one has completed a finite set of require-ments. Secondly, nearly any situation can turn into one that is a challenge to a person's sense of intrinsic moral worth, from something as intimate as a romantic involvement to something as impersonal as an encounter with a store clerk. This, of course, is all in addition to the fact that reading philosophical arguments in this regard will not at all suffice to yield a sense of intrinsic moral worth and the further fact that nothing makes for having a sense of intrinsic moral worth like having the experience of having a sense of intrinsic moral worth.

A different, but hardly irrelevant consideration, is the follow-ing. While it is perhaps true that most mature adults could, were they so to concern themselves, understand Kant or Rawls, it is an unvarnished truth that most individuals in the world do not even have a passing acquaintance with the moral views that either thinker has advanced. Yet, something is surely amiss if we were to conclude that, on account of not having read Kant or Rawls or some other moral theorist, these individuals do not have a sense of moral worth. Most pointedly, we do not want to say that people struggling mightily against injustices do not have a moral sense of worth simply because they have not mastered this or that moral theory.

Taken together, these considerations suggest that a sense of intrinsic moral worth needs a psychological precursor – a psycho-logical mooring, if you will. It should come as no surprise that I take this psychological precursor to be none other than the sense of worth that I have called cherished uniqueness that is bestowed by parental love. To begin with, there are no competing psycho-logical states on the child's part with which parental love has to contend. Quite the contrary, there is nothing to which a child is more receptive than parental love. Hence, where parental love is provided, circumstances favor the child's securing a sense of cherished uniqueness. Second, a sense of cherished uniqueness parallels intrinsic moral worth in precisely the right way. Intrinsic moral worth is not earned. Likewise, cherished uniqueness engendered by parental love is also not earned. The parallel ends here, though, because the grounds for a sense of intrinsic moral worth is simply one's humanity; whereas simply one's humanity is decidedly not grounds for the sense of worth engendered by parental love. Yet, the way in which intrinsic moral worth and cherished uniqueness are parallel to one another enables the latter to serve as a psychological mooring for the former. Neither accomplishments nor appearances nor intellect can be the proper basis for having a sense of intrinsic moral worth. Exactly the same is true for having a sense of cherished uniqueness owing to parental love. Both involve the sentiment that one has self-value independent of one's performances as such. The difference is that in moving from cherished uniqueness to intrinsic moral worth the grounds for self-valuing have shifted as well as the content around which the self-valuing revolves. Regarding the content, the concern of morality is that individuals are not wronged and that they have the space in which to flourish if they so choose. It is not morally incumbent upon individuals to ensure the flourishing of others. With parental love, on the other hand, promoting the flourishing of one's children is among its most fundamental aims – so much so that protecting them from moral wrongs, for all of the importance that attaches to doing so, stands only as parenting's very point of departure. Accordingly, to have a sense of intrinsic moral worth is to have the conviction that others should respect one in various ways; whereas to have a sense of cherished uniqueness is to have the conviction that one's parents are committed to one's flourishing.

Having a sense of cherished uniqueness provides an extraordinarily profound point of departure for having a sense of intrinsic moral worth. For one thing, with a sense of cherished uniqueness in place, the idea of having the proper self-value does not have to begin with morality. Nor, for another, does the experience of being recognized as having self-value begin with morality; for the child has experienced this with the parents. Rather than starting *ex nihilo*, we might think of morality as transforming a sentiment already in place. Whereas parental love bestows upon the child value in the eyes of his parents, not because of what the child does but because she or he is their child, morality extends the idea of having value independent of one's performances. With parental love one should see oneself as having intrinsic worth in the eyes of one's parents; with morality, one should see oneself as having intrinsic worth amidst all human beings. Thus, the intrinsic worth of morality resonates most profoundly with the sense of cherished uniqueness bestowed by parental love. Thus, with cherished uniqueness in place, we have the psychological moorings that render intrinsic moral worth secure.

The view that intrinsic moral worth is in need of psychological moorings might seem odd initially if only because according to rational thought a sense of intrinsic moral worth is an imminently rational state of mind to have. No person could rationally choose to have less than a sense of intrinsic moral worth. This, though, is to confuse the rational desirability of a state of mind with the facility with which one is able to have it. From the fact that a state of mind is rational to have, it by no means follows that it is easy to have that state of mind. It is, for instance, quite rational for airplane passengers to be calm when their flight encounters turbulence, since a plane wreck caused by turbulence alone is extremely rare. Even so, turbulence invariably gives rise to considerable panic among many passengers. There is a fragility that people feel in airplanes, but not in cars, that defies rational reflection, since everyone knows that travel by air is much safer than travel by car. Or consider the sibling who survives a sinking ship, but whose sister dies. There is no rational reason for him to feel unworthy of life, as his sister's death was not related to anything that he did; and he knows this all too well. Moreover, he would be outraged if someone blamed the ship's sinking on him. Even so, what plagues him is the fact that he is alive and she is dead.

So the rationality of having a given state of mind leaves unsettled the facility with which persons can actually have that state of mind. It can be extremely difficult for persons to have the psychological state of mind that they rationally ought to have. The psychological state that constitutes having a sense of intrinsic moral worth is not in any way the exception here. Far from it: The idea that all persons have intrinsic moral worth, and the majestic talk of the Kingdom of Ends associated with this idea, meet with very little affirmation in the daily life of most individuals. Injustice to varying degrees and in various forms abounds; and indifference to injustice abounds. People are quick to see that their own interests have been violated, but are strikingly slow to acknowledge the violation of the interests of others. Even worse, it often turns out that those who know deep oppression first-hand are often blind to the oppression of others. Philosophical arguments, however eloquent, are no match for the harsh reality of experience. With far too many people, the idea of having intrinsic worth radically fails to resonate with so much of their life experiences. Parents take an interest in their children having a sense of cherished uniqueness and in the flourishing of their children; whereas there is no set of persons, corresponding to the role of parents, who take an interest in persons having a sense of intrinsic moral worth.

Much of moral philosophy reads as if it is simply owing to a failure of reasoning that people do not see themselves as having intrinsic moral worth. One would think that all that a person – say our reader of Hill's essay "Servility and Self-Respect" – needs to do is attend sufficiently well to the argument that all human beings have intrinsic worth and then feelings of intrinsic worth will invade her or his being. Accordingly, a person is guilty of defective reasoning in some way by being familiar with the arguments for intrinsic moral worth and failing to have such a sense of worth. So much intellectual ingenuity is spent showing that there is a defect in moral reasoning when people fail to see either themselves or others as having intrinsic worth that what gets ignored is the haunting truth that there is a difference between knowing a simple fact and having an adequate appreciation of it. For example, any foreigner can see that a French note of 100 francs is just that – a French note of 100 francs.[6] This, though, is a very long way from having an appreciation of 100 francs. To have an appreciation of 100 francs is, roughly speaking, to have a sense of its buying power. With 100 francs, a person may reasonably set out to buy milk, bread, mustard, and a jar of coffee – Not, however, a suit or a pair of shoes. Needless to say, an appreciation of the buying power of 100 francs does not follow in the wake of the knowledge that one has 100 francs. This appreciation

---

[6] This example is dated since the euro has replaced most currencies of all countries belonging to the European Union. I have left it in precisely because it illustrates the point rather dramatically – perhaps even more so now. For many of the adult population in France who are over the age of, say, thirty-five, it remains the case that the real value of euros, especially for large sums, is often grasped by converting the sum in question to francs.

would be obtained only by the experience of buying with francs – and not by the ability to convert with lightening speed from one currency into the other. Thus, although the euro has replaced the franc, most of France's adult population grasps the value of euros by converting them to francs; whereas for the foreigner who arrived in France for the first time in January of 2001, it was as if the currency had always been the euro.

By comparison, then, it is most certainly possible for a person to know that she is a human being just like another, and yet fail to have sufficient appreciation of this. Moreover, no amount of ratiocination suffices to deliver that appreciation. The black female slave who suckled the babies of the white slavemaster could not have really doubted her humanity. For neither she nor the master thought that creatures of a different kind could suckle human infants. All the same, she may not have had the feeling of being equal in moral worth to her master even as she routinely engaged in one of the most human of all human activities, namely suckling an infant. Her problem is not that she failed to grasp correctly this or that argument for intrinsic moral worth, but that the sustained treatment she received from the individuals in her social environment, who were invested with power and authority, radically undermined her sense of intrinsic moral self-worth. For the moral significance of suckling went entirely unacknowledged.

It is in this context, then, that we should see the importance of parental love and the sense of cherished uniqueness that it engenders. For persons born in the Kingdom of Ends, coming to have a sense of intrinsic worth would be entirely unproblematic because everyone would always treat everyone in all the morally appropriate ways. But lest it be forgotten, the Kingdom of Ends is nothing more than a heuristic device (albeit an extremely instructive one) for enabling us to understand better our moral standing. The Kingdom of Ends does not speak to the trials and tribulations of viewing oneself as having intrinsic moral worth in an unjust world or, at any rate, in a world that so often can be exceedingly slow to affirm the intrinsic moral worth of its denizens. However valid and sound the argument may be that all human beings have equal intrinsic moral worth, it does not follow that the psychological makeup of individuals must be so constituted.

Parental love, then, provides the grounding for the sense of worth bestowed by moral equality – such love provides the soil, if you will, in which the sense of worth afforded by moral equality may take root. As I have already indicated, I maintain that parental love paves the way for having the proper appreciation of one's moral worth. And it does this by bestowing a sense of cherished uniqueness upon the child without feelings of superiority. It is equally significant in this regard that invidiousness is not an inherent feature of parental love.

To begin with, in expressing their unfailing love for their child, good parents do not in any way diminish the qualities of other children. Nor, to this end, do good parents diminish the qualities of other parents. In fact, precisely what a child typically expects is that other children are loved by their parents just as much as he is loved by his parents; hence, other parents are regarded by the child as good parents as well. No child is ever insecure in her relationship with her parents solely on account of the fact that other children are well loved by their parents. A child can witness a thousand parents showing affection to their children without ever questioning whether he is loved by his parents. What is more, in order for a child to feel profoundly loved by her parents, it is not in any way necessary that she sees her parents giving her more of some good than other parents are giving their children.

If, because other children are being hugged by their parents, a child also wants to be hugged by his parents, it is hardly necessary that this child's parents hug him more than the other parents hug their children in order to reassure him. Nor, in order to reassure him, need they hug him and, in addition, do something further on his behalf. The hug suffices! Thus, children of poor families do not wonder whether they are loved by their parents simply because they do not have the material goods that children of rich families have. The child of poor parents and the child of rich parents could be side by side in the classroom, without the former ever in any way doubting the love that his parents have for him. Nor, for that matter, need the child of the rich parents ever have the thought that her parents love her more than the poor parents love their child.

Needless to say, the obvious but far from trivial truth of the matter is that the non-invidious character of parental love stems from the fact that the basis of parental love is that parents love their children because, and only because, their children are theirs; and it is this foundational conviction that, by their words and deeds, parents generate in their children. Accordingly, differentials between either the parents of other children or the children of other parents are entirely irrelevant. What is more, no child is more or less her parents' child on account of another child being his parents' child.

It is no doubt natural to point out here that the importance that I have attached to parental love hardly applies in all cases, because (for various reasons) it is simply false that people always want the children whom they bring into this world. Pregnancies certainly can be, and sometimes are, unwanted. True enough. As a response, though, two things can be said. The first is that the importance which I have attached to parental love is not at all defeated by the truth that parental love is not always present. Second, I am drawing attention to a distinction in principle between morality and parental love. Even in a morally ideal world as reflected in the Kantian idea of the Kingdom of Ends, parental love would not be otiose; for even in such a world, bringing a human being into the world for the sake of loving it would have no parallel in morality. It is this profound truth concerning parental love of which we must not lose sight. When things are not done properly, things rarely if ever turn out right. Raising a child is no exception to this.

3 PARENTAL LOVE AS A MORAL POWER

I now want to be more precise about the role of cherished uniqueness when it comes to having a sense of moral worth. To state the obvious, it is through the parents that the child first comes to have any sense at all of others acting on that child's behalf. The very wording here is of the utmost importance. For a child does not experience her parents as mere objects of causality who just so happen to give her what she needs; rather, she experiences them as individuals freely expressing their will in acting on her behalf. Born without a sense of self, the child develops it in tandem with the sense that there are those, namely its parents, who choose to act on its behalf. But our choice of actions reveals what we value. If a person freely, deliberately, and regularly chooses A over B, then it follows that this person values A over B. Likewise, if parents freely, deliberately, and regularly act on behalf of their children, then they value their children. Needless to say, however, the difference between a child being valued by its parents and some inanimate object being valued by the same two individuals is that the child experiences being valued by them. Accordingly, the child comes to have a sense of being valued by virtue of the continual experience of being valued by her or his parents.

What is most extraordinary in this regard is that this all occurs pre-linguistically. Long before children are competent speakers of their native language they have a very clear sense that they are valued by their parents. True enough, parents naturally express their affection for their children in a multitude of verbal expressions: "I love you," "You are so precious," "You are our prince(ss)," and so on. Yet even here the desired uptake is secured only if these expressions are uttered in the appropriate way non-verbally. When the words "I love you" are said in a hostile manner, they will not be perceived by the child as affirming.

If things go as they should a child feels wondrously loved by its parents, long before it is has fully grasped the meaning of these utterances. Clearly, if a child's feeling of being loved came only after the child's command of its native language – say, age three or four – enabled it to understand fully utterances such as these, that would already be far too late. The relevance of this point is that the feeling of being valued is secured viscerally before it is grasped in any intellectual way. I shall refer to this as the emotional imprimatur of self-valuing (EISV). It is this EISV that is the foundation upon which moral self-worth sits.

The best psychological evidence available makes it unquestionably clear that the emotional imprimatur of self-valuing is essential on two fronts: (i) it is absolutely essential to the psychological well-being of a child and (ii) it plays a pivotal role in the psychological wholesomeness that a child comes to exhibit later in life as an adult.[7] The philosophical arguments for intrinsic moral

---

[7] It is now common knowledge that systematic child abuse has a lasting impact on the child, bearing mightily upon that child's sense of self in adulthood. For

worth, as well the occasional instances of unambiguous affirmation from others of our having intrinsic moral worth, invariably come too late in the game of psychological development.

It is worth pointing out here that the observation just made holds with equal force with regard to religion. Being a child of the Creator is no doubt an extraordinary thing; and religious leaders, and those who press for social equality, are fond of pointing out that we are all children of the Creator. Indeed, Thomas Jefferson penned the following words in *The Declaration of Independence:* "We hold these truths to be self-evident, that all men are created equal, that they are endowed by their Creator with certain inalienable Rights." These words have yet to lose their majesty. Nor have the riveting words that conclude Martin Luther King's famous speech, "I Have a Dream":

> . . . when we allow freedom to ring . . ., we will be able to speed up that day when all of God's children, black men and white men, Jews and Gentiles, Protestants and Catholics, will be able to join hands and sing in the words of the old Negro spiritual, "Free at last, free at last. Thank God Almighty, we are free at last."

Reference to God invariably stands as a special way of underscoring the idea that each individual is special and unique.

All the same, it is no less true now than it was then that long before a child is able to attach the proper significance to the

a most poignant philosophical discussion of this matter, See Gary Watson, "Responsibility and the Limits of Evil: Variations on a Strawsonian Theme," in Ferdinand Schoeman (ed.), *Responsibility, Character, and the Emotions: New Essays in Moral Psychology* (New York: Cambridge University Press, 1987). I have also discussed the matter in "The Grip of Immorality: Child Abuse and Moral Failure," in J. B. Schneewind (ed.), *Reason, Ethics, and Society* (Chicago: Open Court, 1996).

claim that she or he springs from the Creator and is endowed by Him with certain rights, it is of the utmost importance that a child is loved by its parents. A child's very life would be tragic if this should turn out not to be so. It is important to draw attention to this point only because for the religious the correct moral theory is not Plato's or Mill's or Kant's, but God's. My concern here is not to contest this point. Rather, I merely wish to observe that even if we take it as a given that God exists, it remains true nonetheless that not even God's love, nor therefore God's law, can be a substitute for parental love. If there are any sublime truths in this world, this is surely one of them.

Parental love bestows a sense of cherished uniqueness (without superiority) upon the child; and this, in turn, constitutes an emotional imprimatur of self-valuing on the child's part. This is an emotional imprimatur that has no equal in life, and which is in place long before moral reflection has even begun. Most significantly, this emotional imprimatur is inextricably moral in character. For as the object of its parents' love, precisely what the child learns is that there are morally appropriate and morally inappropriate ways that others may behave toward it; and that this applies with equal force even to those who care mightily for its well-being.

The difference between loving parents and a slavemaster is wondrously instructive here. The slavemaster has an interest in her slaves, and, protects them for this reason. But as every slave would know, being protected by the master from others is perfectly compatible with being roundly abused and mistreated by the master. As a matter of principle, what the master does with a slave is always a matter of whim. Not so, however, with loving parents and their child. Such parents protect their child precisely because they regard him as having independent value;

accordingly, their very protection of him conveys to him that there are limits with respect to what they, as well, may do to him as their child. With children who have been systematically abused, the very problem from the standpoint of protection is that their relationship to their parents is rather like that of the slave to his master. The father who systematically sexually abuses one of his children brings out this point; for he does to his child precisely what would outrage him if another adult were to so treat his child.

Perhaps nothing better illustrates the moral character of the parent-child relationship than the response of parents to the bodies of their children. When the child is an infant, appropriate parental care and love calls for touching every part of its body. As the child grows, the parents take an ever increasing overseer's role in making sure that their child's body is properly cared for; and by the time the child is a young adolescent, the parents generally limit themselves to external "check-points," if you will, such as the face and hair. Washing the genitals of a healthy eleven-year-old is downright unthinkable. These remarks seem so obvious as not to have a point. In fact, though, they speak to the very profound point that, by their behavior, loving parents affirm their moral respect for their child by self-circumscribing, as the child gets older, the ways in which they touch the child's body. The moral sense among adults that their bodies are their own is forged by the parental treatment that each received as a child. This happens, although a philosophical argument is never uttered by the parents nor read by the child as either a child or an adult.

And this gets to the very heart of the matter. Although it is absolutely clear that parents act morally in respecting the bodies of their children, it is equally clear that their motivation for doing so is not so much morality itself, but their love for their children. Only as a joke, and perhaps a cruel one, would parents ever tell their children that we as parents are respecting your body because it is a consequence of such-and-such moral theory that parents are so to behave.

I began this chapter with the claim that a child would not come to have a sense of intrinsic moral worth in the absence of parental love. I have also claimed that parental love is more basic than morality because in the absence of parental love, a sense of moral worth could not obtain a purchase upon our lives. The truth of the second claim follows from the truth of the first. I have already indicated why I take the first claim to be true. Still, it will be useful to make some additional remarks.

It is a conceptual truth that being a child entails being in the formative stages of life, in terms of both physical and psychological development. Accordingly, a fundamental precept regarding human beings is that human development is foundational. What happens at the beginning of life during the pre-reflective years makes an enormous difference during the adult years. This is surely part of the explanation for why systematically abusing and berating a child is wrong. It is not just that these wrongs harm the child at the time of their occurrence, which needless to say is both true enough and horrible enough, it is also the case that these wrongs are formidable impediments to a child's becoming a psychologically whole adult. This general point is so obvious that no one would think to challenge it, although there is disagreement over exactly what follows from it. For instance, some parents think that any form of physical punishment is unjustified; whereas others subscribe to a mild version of "spare the rod; spoil the child."

Rather than entering into this debate, I merely wish to point out that our moral development is also foundational. Even if a psychological attitude itself is not strictly speaking a moral one, this psychological attitude may nonetheless play a fundamental role in both the acquisition and the maintenance of a given moral attitude. The child's belief that it has value in the eyes of its parents independent of its performances is certainly not a moral belief; for it is not all a belief on the child's part regarding how others ought to treat him. Yet, this belief and, of course, the parental behavior that underwrites it, gives rise to a psychological imprimatur on the child's part that is of inestimable value with regard to having the psychological attitude that is constitutive of having a sense of intrinsic moral worth.

Here is why. To begin with, although the idea of intrinsic moral worth is a very elevated and noble one, there is nothing at all innate about it. A person may fail to have this belief even if, as Kantians would insist, it is true that the failure to believe reflects a conceptual flaw in an individual's reasoning. Besides, the truth of a proposition does not entail that it will be believed. Notoriously, there can be psychological obstacles to believing what is true, which brings us to the third consideration. Many beliefs come to be secure in our lives only because they have been roundly and continuously underwritten by experiences. Indeed, the more evaluative the belief is, the more important it is that the belief be underwritten by experience. For example, our belief regarding our physical attractiveness is a highly evaluative one, because it is always vis à vis others that we are more or less physically attractive. Accordingly, it is almost impossible to imagine a sane person failing to believe that he is drop-dead gorgeous if at every turn people are constantly expressing admiration over his looks, wooing him for this or that photo opportunity, and lusting after him at first sight. Likewise, in the absence of ongoing experiences of this sort, it is almost impossible to imagine a sane person believing that he is drop-dead gorgeous.

Now, the belief that one has intrinsic moral worth is also a highly evaluative belief, even though all human beings are said to have such worth. This is precisely because the idea of intrinsic moral worth entails that there is a respect in which all human beings are alike regardless of any and all differences between them. While the idea admits of considerable eloquence, it is not a particularly intuitive one. After all, why should there be one respect in which differences that matter so very much in our lives, and rightly so, turn out not to matter at all? Furthermore, what would make that a plausible way of viewing oneself in a world where differences matter so much? This is where parental love is absolutely pivotal.

Parental love, owing to its constancy over innumerably many differences, experientially grounds in the child the sense that a life can have value independent of appearances and performances, and that a life can have value in the eyes of another without being given over to satisfying that person's wishes. What is more, parental love's efficacy and validity requires neither argument nor understanding at all. There are no doubt deep explanations for why parental love is so efficacious in generating a sense of cherished uniqueness without invidious comparison on the part of the child. All the same, the child does not need to understand any of them in order for this sense of worth to have a deep and abiding place in her or his life. Not only that, when things go as they should, a child's having this sense of worth well in place is not in any way threatened by other children. Thus, when parental love operates as it should in the life of a child, it is in the face of vast differences among children – physical differences as well differences in talent – that the child has a sense of cherished uniqueness, and thus an intrinsic sense of worth.

Parental love, then, can be said to render children psychologically predisposed to take seriously as adults the idea of their intrinsic moral worth, whatever their talents or physical appearances might be and in the face of vast differences among human beings. Indeed, when one fully considers the matters, having such a psychological predisposition is of the utmost importance for the following reason. Although many societies affirm with great rhetorical flourish the ideal that all individuals have intrinsic moral worth, there is very little positive affirmation of this ideal in day-to-day living. This is not because injustice is widespread, but more because it is not the duty of the members of society to provide positive affirmation of the intrinsic moral worth of their fellow citizens. To be sure, the members of society are expected to respect their fellow citizens. However, the respect that is called for here cannot be construed as taking an active role in affirming the moral intrinsic worth of citizens. Rather, the respect called for in this context is best understood as an obligation not to violate the rights of fellow citizens rather than an obligation to act on their behalf to promote their well-being in general and their having a sense of intrinsic moral worth in particular. Accordingly, even in a just society, it could not be expected that a person bereft of a sense of intrinsic moral worth would attain it merely by interacting with people who are occupied with pursing their daily activities.

If, however, a person knew a sense of cherished uniqueness (without superiority) during childhood, then the moral arguments that he has intrinsic worth will resonate mightily with him. They will constitute a new framework with which to extend and deepen his conception of himself. If a person knew a sense of cherished uniqueness from childhood, then he comes to the social community with a deep vantage point from which to see himself as having intrinsic moral worth, even as he understands that his life is no more valuable than anyone else's. Thus, from a psychological point of view he has a reason to take seriously the idea of his having intrinsic moral worth notwithstanding the differences in others that he sees all about him, and notwithstanding the fact that his fellow citizens do not have as their aim as such the promotion of either his well-being or his having a sense of intrinsic moral worth. This is because the ideas embodied in the idea of intrinsic moral worth have their analogue in the intrinsic worth of a sense of cherished uniqueness without invidious comparison. Hence, a childhood filled with a sense of cherished uniqueness is a childhood that gives one a deep readiness for the sense of intrinsic worth that morality offers.

It is an unvarnished truth that life does not always treat people as if they have intrinsic moral worth. In a world fraught with injustice, a person could easily doubt having intrinsic moral worth. The horrific evils of the world reveal that it is perhaps impossible for anyone to have complete immunity to doubts about intrinsic moral worth. But even here we may see a silver lining. For if the cherished uniqueness of parental love makes us so invulnerable to doubt regarding our intrinsic moral worth that it takes an environment like a concentration camp before we can no longer regard ourselves as having such worth, then parental love is surely one of the most precious human virtues the exercise of which proves to be so sustaining.

Parental love is a non-fungible good that provides the emotional imprimatur of self-valuing that makes it possible for the intrinsic worth of morality to have a most secure purchase upon our lives. Without parental love, human beings would have to be constituted very differently for the language of morality as involving a sense of intrinsic worth to be a plausible framework for their lives. Certainly, the way in which human beings begin life would have to be quite different. Given the present configuration of human beings, however: Parental love is a moral power unlike any other.[8]

---

[8] In an important essay, "The Problem of Speaking for Others," *Cultural Critique* 20 (1991–2), written with different matters in mind entirely, Linda M. Alcoff raises important questions about the problem of speaking for others. In precisely the way the love (including parental love) is, I believe that intrinsic moral worth is so profoundly personal that it is a mistake to think that we can fully grasp its imprimatur in another person's life without hearing the individual's account of her or his own life. I failed to appreciate this point when I wrote "Moral Deference" in Cynthia Willett (ed.), *Theorizing Multiculturalism* (Malden, MA: Blackwell Publishers, 1998).

I am very grateful to Thomas Nagel for discussing with me many points in this chapter.

2

Reconceptualizing the Moral Self

The parenting of a child is unique in many ways.[1] One of the most striking of these, however, is that it allows for the fullest expression of unconditional love without in any way failing to respect the child's autonomy. For children, unlike adults, do not have the capacity to be autonomous. If there exists unconditional love in other contexts, the expression of that love must be restrained so as to respect the autonomy of the person who is the object of that love. Children are the perfect vessels for unconditional love. Although born without it, they are marvelously responsive to it. There is no other class of creatures known to humanity that is as responsive to unconditional love as children are. What is more, when children are the object of such love, a nearly immutable foundation is laid for them to become morally

[1] In writing this chapter, I am indebted to a number of pioneers who have written forcefully on the topic of children's rights, parenting, and intimacy. These include: Ferdinand Shoeman, "Rights of Families, Rights of Persons, and the Moral Basis of the Family," *Ethics* 91 (1980); Onora O'Neil, "Children's Rights and Children's Lives," *Ethics* 98 (1988); Jeffrey Blustein, *Parents and Children: The Ethics of the Family* (New York: Oxford University Press, 1982). See also Onora O'Neil and William Ruddick (eds.), *Having Children: Legal and Philosophical Reflections on Parenthood* (New York: Oxford University Press, 1979).

autonomous individuals. Significantly, although there are many marvelous roles that individuals, such as teachers and friends, can play in the life of a child, it is the role of parent that is most suited to bestowing unconditional love upon the child. Parents as such are suited to do this, whatever their station in life might be.

1 PARENTING AS THE FULLEST EXPRESSION OF UNCONDITIONAL LOVE

No matter how much two adults love one another – be it as spouses, siblings, or friends – neither adult is, in the name of that love, justified in imposing her or his conception of the good upon the other. Their expression of love for another must be modulated, as I shall say. This is so even if indeed one adult is correct in her assessment that the other would flourish mightily if only he were to change his ways and pursue the course of action that she counsels; for an adult may respectfully decline the counsel of another even if he has good reason to suspect that she is right. In the name of adventure or whatever, an adult may refuse to do what he suspects is in his best interest. Between adults, the simple truth is that respecting the wishes of one another is, with rare exception, an ineliminable aspect of love at its best, and of their love for one another; and the exceptions prove the rule. When adults fail to respect one another's wishes, they violate one another's autonomy. This brings us back to the parent-child relationship.

Unlike any other human relationship, children allow for the fullest expression of unconditional love by autonomous adult humans; and this, I believe, speaks to why human beings delight in having children. I remarked in chapter 1 that having children is thought to give a completion to life that is not achieved by enormous success in other areas of life. I believe that the opportunity to express unconditional, unmodulated love profoundly speaks to why this is so. It may be thought pets come in second. Perhaps. But surely it is a distant second. This is because pets are incapable of a self-concept that would enable them to understand themselves as being the object of unconditional love, with all that this implies. We know pets can delight in the expression of affection. That, needless to say, is a very long way from them seeing themselves as the object of unconditional love. Suppose that two individuals loved their dog as much as any two parents could love their child. The consequence of this love for their animal would not be an emotional imprimatur of self-valuing. Recall Hume's remark that the minds of men are the mirrors to one another. No dog or cat will ever know that one sacrificed one's vacation, let alone willingly did such a thing, so as not to have to put it in a kennel for ten days. So no pet can ever affirm one for having willingly made a sacrifice of considerable magnitude on its behalf. But a human being can. And the delight that human beings get from affirmation of this kind has no equal among human endeavors. And the parent-child relationship provides a very special conduit for both giving and the affirmation of that giving. The affirmation here is not some form of self-promotion. Rather, it is a kind of proof, if you will, that the good performed on the other's behalf has achieved its intent. Thus, it is rare that good parents seek any form of public recognition for having marvelously raised their children. It typically suffices that the child affirms them in this regard. Here, too, the affirmation does not serve an egotistical concern. Rather, it provides an independent confirmation that only the child can provide.

If this is right, then it would seem that human beings cannot be quite as relentlessly self-interested as theory would have us believe. Let us take a closer look at what is involved in raising a newborn.

Few things are more time consuming than caring for a newborn. The baby has needs, which may manifest themselves at any time during the day or night. And, to put it quite simply, those needs have to be met if that newborn is to survive, and to survive healthily. What is more, the very fragility of a newborn, coupled with its own inability to articulate its concerns or pains, serves only to make the task of parenting all the more demanding. In no time at all, of course, a child comes to have, along with its numerous needs, a host of wants that it can indeed articulate and for which, with great persistence, it can express a desire. Clearly, good parents are those who provide for the needs of the child and navigate through a host of wants, granting some and denying others – in fact, granting some wants at one time and not at another.

Strikingly, much of what I have just said can be said about many other species, too. Or at least the parallel would seem to be close enough. The cubs of a lion, for example, also have needs that must be met, if they are to survive. And lion cubs can be so playful as to endanger themselves; so sometimes their playfulness has to be brought to an abrupt halt. They, too, one might say, have some wants granted and not others; likewise, some wants may be granted at one time and not at another. Undoubtedly, there are a plethora of differences between adult human beings raising human infants and adult members of other species raising their infants. For our purposes, however, the difference to which I should like to draw attention is the following: Only adult human beings can self-reflectively choose to bear children.[2] That is, not only can human beings want to have children, it is also the case that they can want, and be very much content, to have this want. What is more, humans often act on this want with the knowledge that doing so constitutes a tremendous undertaking that may – and often does – call for great sacrifices on their part on behalf of the children. It goes without saying that conceiving a child is not always a matter of choice, a point that held even more so in the past when effective birth control did not exist. None of this, though, counts against the truth that only human beings can self-reflectively choose to have children. Indeed, even in a world of unequal power between women and men, with all that is fulsome and inappropriate about this, a woman could want to have children and want to have this want. As was noted in the introduction, women living under very oppressive conditions have nonetheless wanted to have children. And many women who did not want to conceive and give birth nonetheless adopted the wanted-out-of-love stance when their child was born.

In any case, it simply cannot be said of animals that they self-reflectively choose to have children. Nor, *a fortiori*, can it be said that they do so with the knowledge of the travails that may come about as a result of doing so. For animals simply do not have a self-concept that is sufficiently developed for thoughts of this kind.

Now, a characteristic feature of the project of having children is that this project is conceptually well-informed, but radically task-underdetermined. That is, while the idea of having a child is clear

---

[2] The *locus classicus* of this account of self-reflection is to be found in Harry G. Frankfurt, "Freedom of the Will and the Concept of a Person," *The Journal of Philosophy* 68 (1971).

enough at a sufficiently general level, the details of what raising a child will involve in each particular case is invariably replete with surprises. Everyone is pretty clear about what is involved in bringing a child into the world. Raising and caring for a child, by contrast, is full of unexpectancies. The child may be born with an allergy or a physical disability. Or, despite all efforts to protect it, the child may suffer a physical injury – one that occurs at a most inopportune time in view of other reasonable plans that the family was trying to execute, such as the family vacation. And, of course, the teenage years are typically fraught with one identity crisis after another. Which one will manifest itself, when, where, and how is anyone's guess. And there is no telling whether this or that crisis will require professional intervention. At times, the task of providing food, clothing, and shelter pales mightily in comparison to the enormous emotional and psychological support involved in raising a child.

So it is not just that having a child is costly on a number of fronts, there are three basic unknown variables, namely: when many of the costs will occur, what the costs will be about, and what will be the amount of the costs in each case. In other words, parenting involves making a blanket commitment to acting on another's behalf over an extended period of time. Thus, in self-reflectively choosing to have children, people are self-reflectively choosing to make a blanket commitment to act on behalf of another. This seems to be very much at odds with the idea that human beings are deeply self-interested creatures, where being self-interested is understood as maximizing one's self-interest. Nothing seems more implausible and utterly counterintuitive than the thought that people seek to maximize their self-interest by having children. What is more, let us not forget that having children is not just one of the most common of all human projects, but that it typically has first order of importance among the things that adult human beings want to achieve in their lives. So even if here and there a person might think that having children was a way of maximizing her self-interest, it is clearly out of the question that most people would think this. There is, to be sure, the argument from genetics. However, as we shall see momentarily, that argument does not at all serve the view that having children is a way of maximizing self-interest.

As I remarked in the introduction, folk-wisdom has it that those who have children thereby reveal themselves to be altruistic. When we contrast parenting with the typical instance of altruism, the verdict of folk-wisdom would seem to ring true all the more. Typically, a person is thought to have behaved altruistically simply by virtue of having freely and voluntarily bestowed a benefit upon another without any thought of gaining anything in return. But one can do this without ever making a blanket commitment. Indeed, it is characteristic of most acts of altruism, including those that occasion great admiration, that they do not involve doing anything that remotely resembles making a blanket commitment. Even putting one's very life on the line in order to help another, as majestic and as extraordinary as that is, does not constitute making a blanket commitment. In truth, one can risk one's life in order to save the life of another without ever wanting to be friends with that individual or to have any sort of personal relationship at all with her or him. If someone did such a thing, and then disappeared into the sunset, this would be quite surprising. Yet, she has not on that account done anything wrong, though her behavior is obviously unusual. By contrast, the commitment to having children, precisely because it involves making a blanket commitment, would seem to stand as a most magnificent expression of altruism the occurrence of which is ever so common. Once more, without suggesting that human beings are thoroughgoing altruists, the reality would seem to suggest that human beings have a very deep, even if limited, capacity for altruism, one that exerts a major influence in their lives.

Now, a powerful consideration from a very different direction is the general absence of regret among parents who have had and raised their children, and so among those who are able to look back on their lives and review the decision that they made to do so. Regret is the sentiment that we experience when our assessment of our past choices regarding significant matters reveals that we made a bad choice that was sufficiently costly. Regret is an involuntary sentiment. People who have raised their children are very much in the position to know the resources they spent in doing so, and the opportunities they forwent in doing so. And of course they are aware of their present situation. Admittedly, the question of whether or not one is better off on account of having made a choice cannot always be rigorously assessed. Still, there is often a general sense that people can have nonetheless. At any rate, persons can certainly know whether they are wondrously content in having pursued this or that course of action even if they suspect that they would have been better-off along some dimension – economically, say – had they done something else. There is no incompatibility in being content with being an English professor despite suspecting, and with good reason, that one could have been an extraordinarily successful lawyer with all that this implies in terms of pecuniary benefits.

A quite significant fact, in any case, is that most people do not regret having had and raised their children notwithstanding all the sacrifices involved. The typical claim made by parents who have raised their children is that the experience of parenting is something that they would not trade for anything in the world. No doubt some are self-deceived about this, and perhaps others are exaggerating. However, it is implausible to suppose that the vast majority of individuals are. Another indication of the absence of regret is that people rarely counsel others against having children or at least serve notice that the matter should be given second thought. This often happens when people have had a horrible experience at something. If people were relentlessly self-interested one would expect far more regret from having children than there is. For in terms of opportunities that had to be passed up, there are very few who would not have been able to enjoy a far "richer" life but for the fact that they had children. There is the trip that could have been taken, the hobby that could have been pursued, the marvelous piece of clothing that could have been bought, and so on. It is hard to make sense of relentlessly self-interested people, concerned only with maximizing their self-interest, not feeling regret on account of having to forgo these things. Moreover, the absence of regret here cannot be explained by parents taking comfort in the fact that they did their moral duty. For if doing one's moral duty generally suffices to generate such contentment among individuals who had made such sacrifices on behalf of their children, then, to paraphrase Philippa Foot, these individuals could certainly not have been that self-interested to begin with.[3] Trying to pair the delight that human beings take in having children with the claim that human beings are essentially self-interested is very much like trying to fit a round peg in a square hole. To be sure, parents often find having children gratifying. But those who insist that human beings are self-interested cannot take much delight in this thought. For

---

[3] "Moral Beliefs," in her *Virtues and Vices* (Berkeley: University of California Press, 1976).

one thing, from the truth that having children is gratifying, it does not follow that people have children simply because they are in need of some form of gratification. For another, there is undoubtedly more than one reason why people have children. If it suffices that people have children in order to show them unconditional love, then we do not have a self-interested reason for having children, even if it turns out that the search for gratification is also a factor.

2   Parenting and the Argument from Genes and Self-Interest

I now turn to the view that the self-interest of having children can be grounded in evolution.

Around 1945, there were three billion people inhabiting the earth. That number had doubled by the end of the twentieth century. By 2050, the United Nations predicts that the population of the earth will increase by three billion to nine billion. While this projected figure marks a decrease in the rate of population growth, it still indicates that having children is very much what adults will be doing. Now, of course, there is a very common explanation for why people have children. Alas, it is one that seems to take the altruism out of having children. That explanation is the well-known evolutionary one, namely that people have children in order to pass on their genes. But is it sound?

There is, of course, no gainsaying the evolutionary point that in having children people are doing what is necessary to ensure the survival of their genes. However, this evolutionary point is not what political theorists actually have in mind in claiming that human beings are essentially self-interested. An individual and her or his child are two distinct beings; and the claim of theorists is not that all individuals have a nearly indefeasible interest in the advancement and well-being of their children, but that each distinct being has a nearly indefeasible interest in the advancement of her or his self-interests. One can, to be sure, claim that an individual's children are an extension of her- or himself, a claim that obviously has a point. But the point, such as it is, does not go far enough, since the fact remains that a parent and a child constitute two distinct selves, with the former typically making enormous sacrifices for the latter and not the other way around. And the claim of political theory is that each individual self is fundamentally self-interested. Insofar as self-interest is understood primarily in terms of ensuring the survival of one's genes, it turns out to be a very different notion from what political theorists have in mind in saying that human beings are self-interested. For political theory's conception of self-interest is about persons advancing their well-being as they conceive of it, where the reference is exclusively to each person's own life rather than a life that issues from her or his loins. By contrast, evolutionary theory gives little weight to the self except insofar as the self does what will enable it to ensure the survival of its gene pool. Evolution and political theory are at cross-purposes.

Now, it is often typical of theorists to argue that even if sentiments can be expressed in a manner that does not seem to be self-interested, even altruistic in some instances, these sentiments nonetheless sit upon a very self-interested foundation. Robert Trivers in his seminal essay, "The Evolutional Reciprocal Altruism,"[4] advances this kind of view with great majesty. He

---

[4] *The Quarterly Review of Biology* 46 (1971).

argues that although the moral sentiments such as guilt, remorse, shame, and the like are not self-interested in their expression, they nonetheless turn out to be in our self-interest because they facilitate group reacceptance after one has committed an infraction, which in turn is generally in our self-interest. Hence, so Trivers holds, a self-interested model of evolution shows that the capacity for these sentiments would have been selected for. Accordingly, a self-interested reading of evolution works. Indeed, for the typical person on the street, evolution is often thought to be synonymous with self-interest; and theorists of evolution do precious little to suggest that things are otherwise.

However, it is far from obvious that evolution is committed to self-interest as the deep motivational structure of creatures, humans beings or otherwise.[5] According to evolution, the survival of a species is tied to a very simple principle: Adult members of the species produce progeny that they raise; and these progeny in turn produce progeny that they raise. And so on. The adult

[5] In recent times, no writing has contributed more to the idea that from an evolutionary perspective human beings must be seen as having self-interested motives than Richard Dawkins's *The Selfish Gene* (New York: Oxford University Press, 1989). While reading this amazing book, one has to remind oneself that genes, or replicators, do not themselves think or have group meetings about how to reproduce themselves. More interestingly, perhaps, although the same author makes genes out to be selfish creatures of an intentional kind, he writes the following quite different claim at the end of this book: "It is possible that yet another unique quality of man is a capacity for genuine, disinterested, true altruism. . . . The point I am making now is that, even we look on the dark side and assume that individual man is fundamentally selfish, our conscious foresight – our capacity to simulate the future in imagination – could save us from the worst selfish excess of the blind replicators. . . . We, alone on earth, can rebel against the tyranny of the selfish replicators" (final paragraph of ch. 11, or pp. 200–1 of the 1989 edition). I am indebted to Elliott Sober's marvelous discussion of Dawkins's views at several points. See Sober's *The Nature of Selection* (Cambridge: MIT Press, 1984), chs. 7 and 8.

parents in each case provide sufficient care whereby it is possible for the offspring to become adults in turn. From none of this does it follow that the members of any and all species act out of self-interest at some deep level. The theory of evolution is noncommittal about what it takes to get adult members of a species to produce offspring. And if genuine altruism made the survival of a species more likely than self-interest, there is nothing in evolutionary theory that would require that altruism be jettisoned. There are species that do not care for their offspring at all. Salmon are no doubt the most well-known example of a species that does this. The loggerhead turtle is another one. Salmon leave behind sufficiently many eggs so as to ensure that enough salmon will hatch, reach adulthood, and go on to reproduce in turn. Yet, it would be just plain ludicrous to suppose that (adult) salmon are quite self-interested creatures just looking out for themselves in laying large numbers of eggs. Salmon are just too far down on the evolutionary ladder to have the requiste psychological structure that would permit such a complicated self-interested thought.

In the other direction, bees and ants attend to their larvae with a certain meticulousness. Bees go so far as to ensure that their hive remains at a certain temperature; and so to that end some will serve as living fans. Yet attributing any sort of altruistic motives to either of these insects is surely absurd. For like salmon, ants and bees are too far down on the evolutionary ladder to have the requisite psychological structure that would permit such a complicated altruistic thought. Needless to say, the absence of such a structure is no barrier to the operation of evolutionary theory.

The case of ants and bees is particularly illuminating here because these insects reveal that the theory of kin-selection is not at all about motives.[6] The entire population of a community of either ants or bees shares the same "mother" – the queen; whereas this is absolutely false when it comes to human beings. Even if it is true that creatures are more likely to help the next closest kin, given any two individuals in need, it does not follow that this has anything to do with self-interested motives. Of course, ants and bees lack the requisite psychological structure necessary for having self-interested motives. In general, they cannot on any account be construed as bearing in mind how closely related each member of the colony is to one another, and then act on behalf of one another with that awareness in mind. The forces of evolution are no doubt extraordinary. However, these forces do not require for their operation that there actually be self-interested motives at play. Although evolution applies to all living things on earth, the simple reality is that most living things (such as plants and insects) do not have the requisite psychological structure necessary for motives.

Obviously, the psychological structure of human beings allows for quite complex motives, including self-interested ones. But evolutionary theory does not entail that, in the case of human beings, having children or the desire to have children has to be self-interested in any way. The theory entails only that if the human species is to survive, then human beings had better have children. The theory remains absolutely silent as to the kinds of motives that might best serve achieving this end. And the fact of the matter is that human beings have children for a variety of motives. Some of these motives are absolutely appalling, as when a young teenage girl has a child in order to be liked by

---

[6] The theory of kin-selection was developed by William D. Hamilton, "The Genetic Evolution of Social Behavior," *Journal of Theoretical Biology* 7 (1964).

others or in order to enhance her self-esteem or in order to have someone to love her unconditionally. But there is a more profound consideration of which we should be ever so mindful. If our understanding of human psychology is reasonably accurate, then nothing is more crucial to the psychological development of the child than the constancy of genuine love over a considerable amount of time – years, in fact. Lots of love at a newborn's arrival and sheer indifference thereafter will have an absolutely devastating effect upon the child. Take sustained parental love out of the picture and human survival becomes a nightmare at best and an utter impossibility at worst. Evolution requires that (a) the adult members of a species have the capacity to do what it takes to insure that their progeny can become fit adults who in turn leave behind progeny and (b) this capacity is generally exercised to this end. With salmon this story can be told without love or motives of any sort. Alas, not even an ounce of care is required. With lion cubs, for example, care is essential to their survival. Some measure of psychological warmth over time seems needed as well. By the time we get to chimpanzees, the need on the part of newborn chimpanzees for both care and something resembling affection over time is manifestly obvious. With human beings, the need for both care and affection on the part of the young has its greatest expression. On a most optimistic view of human development, this care and love is needed for at least thirteen or so years. Clearly, nothing serves this end better than a psychological structure that is capable of such a sustained commitment to caring and showing love to another; and there can be no doubt that such a psychological structure is one of the defining features of a human being.

The relevance of this to evolutionary theory is obvious. Surely, the psychological structure of which human beings are capable is not independent of the genetic makeup of human beings, but is inextricably tied to it. Thus, human beings evolved so as to have a genetic makeup that configures a psychological structure that permits such sustained commitment on the part of human beings to the well-being of another. The altruism is in the genes! This altruism does not reduce to self-interest with the observation that the altruism serves the survival of the human species. After all, a regular heartbeat also serves the survival of the human species, as does the capacity to hear. Neither, though, can be explained in terms of self-interested motives or, for that matter, motives of any kind. From an evolutionary point of view, what both wealthy and poor parents have in common is that they can both be equally magnanimous in both caring for and loving their children. Children who are loved by their parents, whether their parents be wealthy or poor parents, have an advantage in life that no other good can afford them. Parental love is a non-fungible good in the parent-child relationship. This in turns makes it a non-fungible good in the very survival of the human species.

To repeat: there is nothing about evolutionary theory that entails that a trait must be self-interested in nature if it serves the survival of the species, or that the members of a community must have self-interested motives. Bees and ants, in particular, show this to be manifestly false. Let us not forget that the vast majority of all living things does not have the psychological capacity to be either self-interested or altruistic; yet, they pass along their genes quite successfully. To insist, then, that we must always have self-interest whenever we have creatures whose psychological structure allows for self-interested motives is to read self-interest into evolutionary theory as opposed to showing that this is a consequence of this theory. In this sense evolutionary theory suffers from bad press. No doubt Charles

Darwin's famous expression "Survival of the fittest" did not help. Alas, people glibly moved from Darwin's view that the more fit individual member of a given species in a given environment is favored to survive over a less fit individual of the same species in that environment to the quite different thesis that individual members of any given species have as their *aim* to outdo the others in order to survive. But Darwin was clear that his views applied to both plants and animals; and he was equally clear that he was not attributing motivations to creatures, writing at one point:

> I should premise that I use this term in a large and metaphorical sense including dependence of one being on another, and including (which is more important) not only the life of the individual, but success in leaving progeny. Two canine animals, in a time of dearth, may be truly said to struggle with each other which shall get food and live. But a plant on the edge of a desert is said to struggle for life against the drought, though more properly it should be said to be dependent on the moisture. A plant which annually produces a thousand seeds, of which only one of an average comes to maturity, may be more truly said to struggle with the plants of the same and other kinds which already clothe the ground. . . . In these several senses, which pass into each other, I use for convenience' sake the general term of Struggle for Existence.[7]

3 Self-Interest As the Best Explanation

Now, there is another reason, quite independent of evolutionary theory and the fact of having children, why the assumption of self-interest has such an appeal among moral philosophers and political theorists, namely the view that if it can be shown that principles of the right (be they moral or political) would be accepted by

---

[7] *Origin of the Species*, chapter 3.

creatures who are assumed to be wholly self-interested, then the suitability of such principles has been established for the most difficult case; hence, the suitability of these principles has been established for all weaker cases where human beings are, to varying degrees, less than wholly self-interested. So on this view, even if it is true that human beings are not essentially self-interested, we might as well assume that they are; and if it turns out that humans are not, then nothing is lost; for if wholly self-interested persons would adopt and adhere to a given set of principles, then *a fortiori* less self-interested people would do. Hence, the assumption of self-interest is philosophically innocent. Let us refer to this as the dominance argument.[8]

The dominance argument seems so intuitively right that very few think to question it. Yet, the argument is woefully problematic. One reason why this is so is that the dominance argument cannot capture what many find admirable and ennobling about living an upright life. It certainly cannot be thought that an upright person begrudgingly does what is right, and that she or he views principles of the right as a necessary burden.

According to the dominance argument, (1) the demands of principles of the right are best understood as nothing more than burdensome restrictions upon the complete freedom of persons to advance their self-interests – something which persons are held as being naturally inclined to do. So (2) if it would be rational for completely self-interested individuals to accept a set of restrictions on the freedom to advance their self-interests, then surely it would be rational for less self-interested individuals to do so. And from these considerations, it is thought to follow that

---

[8] David Gauthier is one of the foremost proponents of the dominance argument. See his *Morals By Agreement* (New York: Oxford University Press, 1986).

(3) it is irrelevant to moral and political theory construction if human beings turn out to have a less self-interested nature, since the less self-interested persons necessarily have their situation covered by the more self-interested type.

Alas, even if we grant (1) and allow that (2) follows from (1), it is false that (3) thereby follows. Essentially, this third claim begs the question regarding motives; for it follows only if the motives that people have for adhering to principles of the right are irrelevant. This is not so, however. Even if it is true that both purely self-interested and wholly altruistic individuals would embrace the same principles of the right, what does not at all follow is that their motives for doing so would be the same. By hypothesis, each self-interested individual would embrace a set of principles of the right because and only because he could not otherwise do better for *himself*; whereas this could not possibly be the explanation for why each altruistic person would embrace the same principles. What is more, while self-interested individuals might have no qualms whatsoever in having the motives of altruistic individuals attributed to them, as we learn from Thrasymachus in Plato's *Republic*, the converse is most certainly false. The altruistic person may not flaunt the good that she or he does for others. This, however, is not tantamount to her being indifferent to others attributing untoward motives to her. A person may not want the world to know that she gave mightily to a worthy charity such as the Red Cross, from which it does not follow at all that she is indifferent to others thinking that she stole from that charity.

To ignore the motives with which persons might adhere to principles of the right is to ignore one of the essential features of human beings, namely their capacity to act from a variety of complex motivational structures even when they exhibit the same kind of behavior. Suppose three students study most assiduously for an examination. The first does so because of her love for the subject; the second does so because he will fail the course if he does not pass this examination; and the third, who does not even need the course, does so because she wants to prove to others that Latino students are just as good at mathematics as any other student. No one would dare suggest that we might as well assume that the motivation of any one of these applies to all three. Not only that, the differences in motivation are important to how we understand each of them as a person. Even if the first and the third students are viewed as admirable for studying so assiduously, the grounds for that admiration differ between them. And if the second student can be admired for finally applying himself, the grounds for that admiration are different yet again. The only way to pass the examination is to study; yet, this truth does not at all obliterate quite important differences in motivational structure between these three individuals, though it should turn out that we have exactly the same study behavior among them. For all we know, they are friends who study together.

Even if it is allowed that the dominance argument can tell us what principles of the right are viable, what the argument cannot tell us is why persons might adhere to those principles. And one should not, and in reality cannot, ignore the difference between those who begrudgingly accept a set of principles of the right and those who embrace such principles as an admirable ideal. Why? Because it is precisely upon this difference that trust turns. A person who begrudgingly accepts principles of the right is far less trustworthy, if at all, than is the person who embraces these same principles as an ideal. This is because persons are trustworthy only if they can be counted on to do their part even if they get could get away with not doing so at little or no cost to themselves. By definition a person who begrudgingly accepts principles of the right cannot be counted on in this way; whereas one who embraces such principles can. It is easy to miss this if one focuses only upon the outcome; for we can have the same outcome with both a trustworthy person and an untrustworthy person. For example, if everything in one's home is under lock and key, then with respect to stealing we will have the same outcome between the trustworthy visitor and the untrustworthy one, in that neither will steal anything. Just so, the difference between the two is extraordinary. No rational person could be indifferent to whether a visitor in his home is trustworthy or not. With the trustworthy visitor, it holds that she would not have stolen anything even if nothing had been under lock and key; whereas this is precisely what does not hold with the untrustworthy one. Although circumstances may be such that we can predict the same outcome whether a person is trustworthy or not, what does not follow in the least is that the difference between a trustworthy person and an untrustworthy one is null and void.

Here is a more vivid illustration of this point. Notwithstanding the crime rate in the United States, the truth of the matter is that most people can predict that they will get through the day without being murdered. It is obviously the case that, on any given day, most people are not murdered. Now we can ask, on the basis of what is this prediction possible? Needless to say, effective law enforcement is not the answer. There could not be enough law officers for that. And even if there could be, the question that immediately arises is why is it that law officers, having the cover of the badge, do not commit murder. True, most murderers are apprehended. However, this is due to the fact that in comparison to the size of the population the percentage of murders that take place is minuscule. If at any given point in time most members of the population were to decide to murder someone, there is very little that could be done to prevent such a calamity. So the prediction that most people will not be murdered is based upon what? The answer, perhaps surprisingly, is the simple fact that most people do not want to murder anyone, and would not do so even if they could commit murder with total impunity. In other words, it is not that most people begrudgingly refrain from committing murder. Rather, it is that most people have no desire whatsoever to commit such a deed. In this regard, then, most people are *trustworthy*.

As I have indicated, it is really not possible to have a law enforcement situation that is so effective that for the most part this is the only reason why people refrain from committing murder. But if it were, then society would be a nightmare. This is because social tranquility is ineluctably tied to the belief that we are able to trust most members of society not to commit murder.

In a society, then, what we want by and large are not individuals who begrudgingly comply with principles of the right, but individuals who embrace such principles. Indeed, in a just society it is the latter and only the latter that will be true. Thus, it is simply a mistake to hold that even if individuals are not in fact essentially self-interested, it is just fine to assume that they are for the sake of argument.

No doubt it is tempting to think that history itself lends considerable support to the presupposition of the dominance argument that human beings are essentially self-interested. I think not, however. Far from pointing to just how self-interested human beings are, history reveals just how capable human beings are of holding not just false beliefs, but unwarranted false beliefs, even some that defy common sense and so *a fortiori* beliefs that are irrational. The distinction between false beliefs and unwarranted beliefs is extremely important. Consider, for instance, the belief that the earth went around the sun has always been false. As we know, it certainly has always been the other way around. However, 2000 years ago, it was rational to believe that this is what happened. Indeed, in the absence of a theory of gravity and kinematics, it would actually have been irrational to believe what in fact has always been true, namely that the earth goes around the sun. Accordingly, the belief that the sun went around the earth was a false belief. It was not, however, an unwarranted false belief. Likewise for the belief that dolphins and whales were merely big fish. This is the belief that people held regarding these mammals a thousand or so years ago. The belief was false, but not unwarranted given the biological knowledge that people possessed at the time, and given both the appearances of these two mammals and the fact that their home is the sea. Painfully, there has been no shortage of unwarranted false beliefs among human beings.

From the Crusades to the Salem witch hunts,[9] history reveals that human beings have been enormously animated by unwarranted false beliefs about other human beings. Christians have believed that Jews were demons and that they sacrificed gentile children. Other Christians have taken the slightest aberration in behavior – including prolonged illness upon occasion – as evidence that a person was possessed by a demon, and in some instances was an actual ally of Satan. Individuals so viewed, typically females, were called witches. What is more, a punishment was meted out that put the accused in a no-win situation. Thus,

---

[9] See, e.g., Joshua Trachtenberg, *The Devil and the Jews: The Conception of the Medieval Jew* (Philadelphia, PA: The Jewish Publication Society, 1988) and Peter Charles Hoffer, *The Salem Witchcraft Trials* (University of Kansas Press, 1997).

an accused might be thrown into a pond with the following understanding: On the one hand, her drowning, and so her death, proved that her soul had been purchased by the devil; on the other, her survival, alas, was proof par excellence that she was one of Satan's cohorts. Very poor whites have believed that they were, by virtue of the color of their skin, superior to blacks; and recently, some blacks have returned the compliment, as it were, insisting that all things good and true originated in Africa. Men have believed in the intellectual inferiority of women simply because they were female. The list goes on. The unwarranted false beliefs that many have held dear are often stupefying.

The history of human conflict reveals human beings as extremely susceptible to unwarranted false believes about other humans and quite capable of acting upon them. That self-interest has been served in some of these instances has sometimes been more of an unintended consequence rather than an outcome of rational behavior. If history is to serve as our guide, any belief in the rational economic person had better be taken with one incredibly large grain of salt. For not only have people doggedly held beliefs that have defied all common sense, but people have also acted on these beliefs at enormous costs to themselves, both emotionally and economically. In the aim of exterminating Jews, Hitler wrought even further havoc upon the German economy – the very thing that he sought to revive with his virulent anti-Semitic rhetoric. Maintaining plantations of black slaves was not obviously cheaper than hiring poor whites, since there were no minimum wage constraints during slavery. Yet, white people were committed to this exceedingly risky arrangement nonetheless. Plantations spoke to a certain ideological conception of the self. They did not constitute an eminently rational choice from an economical point of view. Indeed, one of the striking things about all forms of prejudices is just how phenomenally irrational they can be, how much they can fly in the face of self-interest. When one considers, then, the extent to which throughout history irrational prejudices have been the basis for ever so costly wars, the world's history of wars hardly provides a basis for supposing that persons are self-interested. Instead, this history would seem to suggest that persons will often remain committed to their ideologies even when doing so is manifestly at odds with their self-interest. To be sure, there have been battles driven by self-interest alone. I have hardly denied this. There is no need to deny this, if only because sometimes leaders have rallied their citizens by exploiting unwarranted false beliefs that the general population held regarding those to be attacked. As we all know from contemporary politics, a good epithet can be more effective in galvanizing an audience than a wealth of solid arguments could ever hope to be. A most striking thing about the world is that we get very little of the cooperation among individuals to which the mere pursuit of self-interest would give rise. In every corner of the earth one finds that ideological commitments have a much greater hold on individuals than self-interest generally has ever had.

Before returning to the moral significance of parenting, I should like to briefly take up one more consideration that is often thought to lend credence to the dominance argument, namely the story of Robinson Crusoe.

4 A Supposed Lesson from Robinson Crusoe

Philosophers are fond of the story of Robinson Crusoe, noting that if a person were left deserted on an island, he would naturally and unabashedly seek to advance his self-interests in all that he did.[10] Hence, so the argument goes, this shows that human beings are naturally self-interested. The problem here is that we have an argument whose validity seems plausible, but whose soundness is in doubt because the truth of the argument's premise is very much open to question. First of all, notice that if being self-interested is to be contrasted with being altruistic, there is the conceptual truth that it is not possible for Robinson Crusoe to be altruistic, since there is no one around upon whom he can bestow a benefit without thought of gaining something in return. That is, he could not choose to be altruistic even if he wanted so to behave. Even a Mother Teresa, the very embodiment of altruistic ideals, would not have been able to act altruistically were she stranded on a desert island. Indeed, while such a person could commit suicide, she could not risk her life in order to save another's life. This should give us pause. For if a person is situated so that it is conceptually impossible for her or him to act altruistically, then it is also conceptually impossible for that very same individual to act in a self-interested manner. Upon reflection, this should come as no surprise; for the self-interested person is not simply one who does what will make her or him better off, but the individual who does so with enormous, if not complete, disregard for others. However, it is impossible to have such disregard for others on a desert island. This truth is not defeated by the quite reasonable presupposition that Robinson Crusoe naturally does whatever will make him happy while all alone on

---

[10] In writing this section, I am much indebted to the distinction drawn by Stephen Darwall, *Welfare and Rational Care* (Princeton University Press, 2002), between interest and being in one's interest, ch. 2; John Conlisk, "Why Bounded Rationality?," *Journal of Economic Literature* 34 (1996); and Kristen Renwick Monroe, "A Fat Lady in a Corset: Altruism and Social Theory," *American Journal of Political Science* 38 (1994).

the island. For though he does this with the aim of bringing comfort and contentment to himself, he does not so behave with the aim of having more than others of any given good or even with the aim of preventing others from having whatever it is that he has. On a desert island, Robinson Crusoe cannot rationally have either aim.

Nor is there any reason to think that a Robinson Crusoe would be interested in merely accumulating things as such – say as much wood as possible or as much stone as possible – simply for the sake of having as much of whatever it is as possible. For this is to turn accumulation into a kind of fetish. On a desert island, one needs wood, for example, to build artifacts (a house or a table) or a fire. It would be reasonable to accumulate ample wood for these purposes. In the absence of a story, though, Robinson Crusoe would not have a reason to stockpile wood as such, simply to have mounds of wood here and there. Just having mounds of wood sitting around, far from being imminently rational, is just downright silly. Besides, if the entire island is at his disposal, then the idea of maximization as such is incoherent.

Many take the case of Robinson Crusoe as a way of establishing a metaphysical or conceptual truth about the motivational structure of human beings, namely that human beings do what is in their self-interest; for surely this is the case with Crusoe. Let us concede for the sake of argument that Crusoe's desert island behavior counts as self-interested behavior. This turns out to be only a Pyrrhic victory, as the following example will show. Imagine that Susie gathers a barrel of water for herself fully aware of the fact that there is more than enough water for anyone else so moved to do the same. Let us call this considerate self-interest. Now imagine a very different scenario in which John gathers a barrel of water for himself. The difference is that John gathers his water knowing full well that there will be no more water left for anyone. Let us call this *inconsiderate* self-interest. Needless to say, considerate self-interest does not entail inconsiderate self-interest. That is, from the knowledge that a person would gather water for herself given that there is plenty left for everyone else, we cannot thereby infer that this person would gather water for herself if she knew that there would be no water left for anyone else to use. It is, of course, inconsiderate self-interest that theorists have in mind when they say that human beings are self-interested. And inconsiderate self-interest is not established by the Robinson Crusoe scenario – at least not without an awful lot of additional and controversial premises.

This brings us to a point that serves as a fitting conclusion for our discussion of Robinson Crusoe. How people behave under quite unusual circumstances often does not reveal much about how they will behave under typical circumstances. Under extreme circumstances, people have been known to scrounge through feces in search of a mere morsel of nourishment. Faced with starvation and stranded far away from civilization, people have reluctantly consumed the flesh of the dead around them. Clearly, people are not inclined to behave this way generally. So even if it is allowed for the sake of argument that Robinson Crusoe acting alone on a deserted island would exhibit nothing but (inconsiderate) self-interested behavior (contrary to what I have established), it does not thereby follow that this is how people situated in society would behave.

5 Parenting as an Open-Ended Commitment

Let us return now to that most common of all human activities, namely having children and parenting. Needless to say, the

majesty of parenting hardly lies in the fact that parents provide for the basic needs of their child. This, to be sure, is far
from being a trivial task. Still, accomplishing this task cannot be
what makes parenting so profoundly rewarding. After all, adult
children sometimes do this for their elderly parents who have
become weak and feeble; yet, no one thinks for a moment that
adult children meeting the basic needs of their elderly parents is
parallel in any way whatsoever to the majesty of parenting. The
former is often characterized as a burden that one must bear.
Even elderly parents themselves often speak of not wanting to be
a burden to their children. By contrast, the presumptions that
come with parenting a child are at the opposite end of the spec-
trum. Parenting a child is generally seen as an extraordinarily
marvelous experience, notwithstanding all the vicissitudes that
come with doing so. With very rare exception, those who claim
otherwise are thought to have gotten something terribly wrong.
Even parents whose child has severe birth defects are reluctant
to characterize caring for the child as a burden, though many
are in awe of parents who do so with unfailing tranquility. How is
the difference between parenting a child and caring for elderly
parents to be explained?

As it happens, the answer is surprisingly simple. The essence
of parenting, beyond meeting the basic needs, lies in endowing
the child with a conception of the good that achieves fruition.
This is why parental pride in a child has no equal, no matter how
proud others (such as teachers and other adult role models) may
be of a child's successes. For the parents are the ones who, at the
most fundamental level, made it possible for the child to have
a conception of the good that, in turn, achieved fruition. The
support and encouragement of others is an embellishment only,
and never the scaffold. This reality is one reason why people

are so eager for adoptions at birth; for then it is they and they alone who constitute the foundation for the child's conception of the good. Again, this is why parents can be proud of the success of their child, even if they have little or no understanding of exactly what it is that the child does. There are numerous stories of parents beaming with untold joy over their child's first book, although the book could just as easily have been written in another language when it comes to what parents can understand from reading the book. It is significant that no child in the situation that I have just described thinks that the parental pride is somehow false, since the parents cannot understand the contents of the book. This is because that reality does not detract one iota from the fact that the parents played an indisputable foundational role in the child's coming to have a conception of the good that, in turn, reached fruition.

Bringing it about that a child has a conception of the good that, in turn, reaches fruition. This is the essence of parenting and the expression of what I call unmodulated altruism. And most people attach more importance to realizing this twin-ideal than they do to realizing any other ideal that they might have in life. Realizing this twin-ideal is held to render their life complete in a way that nothing else possibly could. When this consideration is coupled with the two main arguments of this chapter concerning evolutionary theory, on the one hand, and the Robinson Crusoe story, on the other, the thesis that human beings are essentially and inescapably self-interested does not ring true at all. For that thesis is understood to mean that there is nothing that is more characteristic of the motivational structure of human beings than the desire to maximize their self-interest by acquiring some good or surpassing others in some way. Needless to say, parenting is nothing like that at all.

A final comment. One might have thought that what human beings most want is to lead a meaningful life. And it is a striking fact that nature has been radically egalitarian and supportive in this regard; for raising children is one of the ways in which human beings generally can lead a meaningful life regardless of how they are socially situated. Not because nothing else is important in life except raising children, but because nothing else is *as* important as doing so. This accords with modernity's most important contribution that all human life is sacred. Surely, the helpless new life that we bring into the world is no less sacred. And evolutionary theory as it applies to human beings would seem to tell us just that.

The inclination for unmodulated altruism is a profound feature about human beings. Alas, much political and moral theorizing has either denied this feature about humanity or assumed it away for the sake of theoretical eloquence. A strong impulse for unmodulated altruism, even where it involves one's progeny, constitutes a level of altruism that far exceeds what one might expect given the assumption that human beings are essentially self-interested creatures.

With much contemporary moral and political theory, the concern is to obtain altruistic behavior out of a self-interested motivational structure. For it is assumed that the primary concern of individuals is to maximize their self-interests; hence, the projects that humans pursue are to be understood in this way. I have shown in this chapter that this view of things is not in keeping with the fact, as indicated by what people say and do, that the project of having children is considered by many to be the most significant and meaningful endeavor in their lives. I have hardly argued that people do not act in significant self-interested ways, as it is obvious that they do. Rather, I have argued simply that the importance and significance that people attach to having children shows that it is a mistake to think of human beings as relentlessly self-interested. This is because the project of having children can only be understood as a remarkably altruistic endeavor, notwithstanding the fact that the object of this altruism is none other than the very offspring of individuals. It has seemed to many that unvarnished self-interest can be harnessed for moral ends. The philosophical question since Hobbes has been: What moral and political principles best serve the interests of wholly self-interested persons?[11] It may very well be that we must not lose sight of the self-interested impulse of human beings. Just so, the arguments in this chapter suggest another way in which we might proceed, namely by harnessing the manifest altruism of individuals that is revealed in their deliberately and voluntarily having children. What light does this altruistic fact about humanity shed upon what a society should be like? I take up this concern in Part 2 of this book.

[11] For one of the most distinguished contemporary accounts of Thomas Hobbes available, see Jean Hampton, *Hobbes and the Social Contract Tradition* (Cambridge University Press, 1986).

Part II

The Crucible of Society

3

The Family as a Model for Society

R ecall Rousseau's striking comparison that was mentioned in the introduction to this book:

> The family is the first model of political societies. The head of soci-
> ety corresponds to the position of the father; whereas the people,
> themselves, correspond to the image of the children. What is more,
> all are born equal. . . . The only difference is that with the family,
> the love of the father for his children is what, as it were, rewards him
> for that which he does on their behalf. (*Social Contract* Bk I, Ch. 2)

My aim in this chapter is to make good Rousseau's striking claim that the family serves, not only as a model for society, but as the first model, by delineating several ways in which raising children has important parallels in a just society.[1] A caveat is in order. We

---

[1] In writing this chapter, I have been very mindful of Martha Nussbaum's important work *Women and Human Development* (New York: Cambridge University
Press, 2000). Rousseau, like most thinkers at that time, did not have an egalitarian view of women. However, it is with an egalitarian view of women and men
that I write. See Elizabeth S. Anderson, "What is the Point of Equality?," *Ethics*
109 (1999). What impresses me about the latter's account is the objectivity that
she explicitly embraces when it comes to human flourishing. Regarding democratic equality, she writes: "It conceives of justice as a matter of obligations that
are not defined by the satisfaction of subjective preferences" (p. 336).

do not characteristically refer to the family as just. Instead, it is usually characterized as loving or not. So strictly speaking, the parallel is between a loving family and a just society. As we shall see, however, this parallel is more apt than one might initially suppose, because society has an analogue to parental love and the family has an analogue to rights.

1 SOME PRELIMINARY REMARKS

Although Rousseau never really defends the claim that the family serves as a model for society, there can be little doubt that he intended it. For this comparison is taken from Chapter 5 of the first edition of *The Social Contract* and restated it with greater eloquence, perspicacity, and force in Chapter 2 of the second edition of that work. However, we tend not to defend what we take to be obvious, even if the obvious is of great importance. Centuries ago, and even at the beginning of the twentieth century, the thesis that all human beings are equal was a controversial one that required considerable argument. Not so, nowadays. The equality of all human beings is taken as an obvious and fundamental truth – a point of departure – upon which an argument may build. The United Nations *Declaration of Human Rights* has become a fixed point of reference.[2] Yet the thesis that all human beings are equal with respect to fundamental moral and political rights is hardly a trivial one. Quite the contrary, this assumed thesis is routinely appealed to these days. So Rousseau's opening remarks in *The Social Contract* that liberty is natural for *all* human beings was quite radical for his time. This is because at

[2] For a wonderfully sensitive discussion concerning the value of rights, see Kenneth Baynes, "Rights as Critique and the Critique of Rights," *Political Theory* 28 (2000).

the time of Rousseau's writing, slavery already had a very long history, from Aristotle on through the Islamic Empire.[3] Indeed, it is Aristotle's view regarding the naturalness of slavery that Rousseau explicitly addresses.

At any rate, if the comparison of society to family was obvious when Rousseau made it, the comparison is far from obvious today. So let me frame the argument for this chapter.

My focus in this chapter will be on raising children. Thus, I will attend to parents as adults and their relations only insofar as this bears upon raising children. I shall assume throughout the discussion that parents have at least two children because this brings out issues related to society that do not arise in the case of an only child. There is no implication, implicit or otherwise, that an only child is in any way worse off (or, for that matter, better off) than children with siblings in terms of either moral or psychological development. Yet, when it comes to parenting, the assumption of more than one child serves to mirror the idea of justice among equals on two accounts: on the one hand, the parents are equals to one another; on the other, the children are equals to one another, though children are never the equal of their parents – at least not for some time to come. It is obvious that for Rousseau children are parallel to citizens and parents are parallel to the governing authority of society. To be sure, Rousseau wrote at a time when men "ruled" the household, and so ruled both women and children. Thus strictly speaking

---

3 Thus, there is no reason whatsoever to believe that Rousseau wrote his remarks about slavery with American slavery in mind. Regarding Islamic slavery, see Shaun E. Marmon (ed.), *Slavery in the Islamic Middle East* (Princeton, NJ: Marcus Weiner Publishers, 1999). For a most important discussion concerning moral objectivity with respect to social injustices, see Michele Moody-Adams, *Fieldwork in Familiar Places* (Cambridge: Harvard University Press, 1997).

the parallel for Rousseau is between father and the governing authority of society, as he indicates in the quotation with which I began this chapter. However, there is no reason to think that the parallel between family and society that Rousseau envisaged holds only if men rule in both home and society. What is more, if the parallel holds in spite of a more egalitarian view regarding women and men, then that speaks to its efficacy.

Of course, the very notion of the family is anything but rigid these days.[4] Perhaps it was never rigid. The adult members of a family may include aunts and uncles or grandparents or even godparents. Or, this may be extended to include neighbors who, in some instances, are given the honorific title of aunt or uncle. Each individual may play more or less of a role in parenting. For simplicity's sake, though, the discussion will be cast in terms of two parents. These two individuals may be biological parents or not. Or they may be of the same gender. What is of the moment for our purposes is not how individuals came to have the role of parents in the life of a child or what the gender or sexual orientation of the parents might be, but the simple fact that the individuals in question are the parents. For the duties that come with parenting or the general structure of parenting does not change depending on whether one is the biological parent or not or whether one is of one gender rather than another or whether one has this or that sexual orientation. Nor is there any reason to think that these contingencies bear upon the where-withal to fulfill these duties. Persons who cannot fulfill the duties of parenting should not have or adopt children, regardless of the

---

4 See James Walker and Nick Stinnett, "Parent-Child Relationships: A Decade Review of Research," *Journal of Marriage and the Family* 33 (1971), for an interesting and important discussion of the family.

biological or social categories in which they may or may not fall, by either their own measure or the measure of others. Still, for simplicity's sake, yet again, the discussion shall be cast in terms of female and male as mother and father, respectively, and in terms of a spousal relationship.

For some, this may be tantamount to valorizing the family as heterosexual. That, however, is not my aim. Instead, I want to draw attention to the character of the parent-child relationship by valorizing certain responsibilities that parents have toward children. Although I assume it to be true that good parenting has nothing to do with either gender or sexual orientation, I am not defending that thesis here; and casting the argument in terms of female and male as mother and father, respectively, allows the argument to proceed without having to attend to complexities that might pertain to same-sex parenting, either by speaking to these complexities or by arguing that they are more apparent than real. It goes without saying that a book that spoke to these matters would be a very important contribution to our thinking about parenting; and that is precisely the reason why I shall not, and should not, pretend that I am doing so in this work.

2   PARENTAL LOVE AND CONCEPTION OF THE RIGHT

I begin the argument to illustrate the parallel between parents and society in two ways. In this section, I shall argue for the importance of a conception of the right in the family. Then in the next section I shall argue for the importance of general goodwill in society, where general goodwill is to be understood as the parallel to parental love.

Minimally, a conception of the right implies that there can be behavior that is either obligatory or impermissible, where

the grounds for this admit of a justification that is independent of mere wishes and preferences that individuals might have.
Accordingly, a piece of behavior can be obligatory although the
person does not wish to engage in it; or conversely, it can be
impermissible although the person very much wants so to behave.
In moral theory, there is much debate over whether the right
is prior to the good; and, in particular, whether acting out of
love reflects the proper moral motivation for doing what is right.
Whatever the general outcome of this debate, the family can be
as it should be only if the sentiment of love and the conception
of the right operate in tandem, provided that parental love, the
good in this case, seeks to operate in accordance with the right,
and the right is animated by parental love. Parental love has
motivational priority; whereas the right has epistemic priority. It
seems to me that much contemporary discussion has missed the
distinction between whether the right or the good has priority.

Although love is a most powerful and important sentiment
in human relations, it is neither a conception of the truth nor a
conception of the right. Love in and of itself is neither knowledge
about how to live nor knowledge about what is good for the other;
rather, love is informed by knowledge regarding these matters,
be it moral, scientific, or practical. One can love a person and
yet grasp incorrectly what his ailments or problems are, or be
misinformed about what the appropriate solutions to them are.
Similarly, one can love a person and be mistaken about what is
the morally correct action to take with respect to her situation or
behavior. We can, for instance, certainly be mistaken regarding
how to respond to the moral pain of another.

As remarked in chapter 1, psychology has given us an understanding of children that was unavailable to folks hundreds of
years ago. It has always been assumed that parents should love

their children, but it is only with psychology that we have an appreciation for the importance of constancy of parental affection in an infant's life. Thus, regularly leaving a newborn infant in the hands of strangers for days on end is something that parents not only should have difficulty doing because they so love the child, but also should realize it is in fact utterly inimical to the psychological development of the child. And this makes such parental behavior morally objectionable. This specific moral conclusion would not have been warranted hundreds of years ago, as the facts were simply not there to support it. Or, to take a different example, violence between parents has no place in the home. But we know now that the behavioral patterns of children are influenced by regularly witnessing violent behavior between parents. This gives a certain urgency to parents not acting violently before their children.

Unlike people in previous centuries, we now know that the ways in which an individual is regularly treated by his parents during his childhood may have a most significant impact on the psychological development of that individual's personality, and that the frequent violation of trust at a tender age is apt to have an absolutely devastating impact on the child later as an adult, as the case of child sexual abuse so poignantly shows. In particular, we know that it is a mistake to think that a child will turn out just fine despite childhood trauma if everything is as it should be later on in life. All the same, it is surely false that hundreds of years ago parents did not love their children as much as parents do nowadays. Rather, through no fault of their own, those parents were far less informed about the psychological wherewithal of children.

Finally in this regard, consider the biblical injunction "Spare the rod, spoil the child." Invoking this biblical reference, time was when many held that corporal punishment served a child well. Nowadays, however, many reject this view on the grounds that inflicting corporal punishment on a child is thought to be harmful to its psychological well-being.[5] Furthermore, corporal punishment is thought to teach the wrong moral example to the child regarding the use of force. So, while a light and occasional spanking on a child's rump is acceptable to enough parents, we fully reject the old days when a child was sent to the shed for a sustained whipping with a rope or a branch.

Love, then, is not enough when it comes to being good parents. Knowledge is indispensable; and this knowledge includes a conception of the right. At first glance, this point might seem to be quite at odds with the argument presented in chapter 1, where I argued that parental love provides a sense of uniqueness without invidious comparison. Not so, however. The idea is that love is the reason why one does what is right; and it is this truth that is conveyed to the child. Love is the answer to the child's question "Why do you want to treat me in the right way?" And to that question love can be the only acceptable answer. However, the motivational primacy of love, far from negating the right, creates a space for it – and necessarily so. Part of what is involved in loving another is conveying to that individual that there are things that are in point of fact good for her and, therefore, that the good for her is not simply a matter of whim. Love is incompatible with the arbitrary treatment of another; and the only way for love to be nonarbitrary is that it is anchored in a conception of the right. By contrast, the only way for treating a child in accordance with a

---

5 For a discussion of this subject, see P. Greven, *Spare the Child: The Religious Roots of Punishment and the Impact of Physical Abuse* (New York: Random House, 1991).

conception of the right, without seeming as if it were a burden, is for acting in accordance with the right to be animated by love. So, contrary to what some have supposed, there is no formal incompatibility between acting in accordance with love and acting in accordance with a conception of the right.[6] The marvelous moral lesson taught to children is that because they are loved it is right to treat them in some ways and wrong to treat them in others. Strikingly, so many discussions in moral and political thought miss the simple truth that we begin our lives experiencing both love and a concept of the right in tandem, rather than as two competing claims upon our lives. Indeed, one of the most sublime lessons that children come to grasp in the fullness of time, when things proceed as they should, is that sometimes parental love necessitates chastisement, which is a way not just of expressing disapproval but of underscoring the importance of the right.

It is not enough to observe that the very nature of love is such that it seeks to identify with the good of the loved-one. For as we have just noted this truth alone leaves unanswered the question "What is good for the loved-one?" What parents cannot say, at least not if they are good parents, is that it does not matter what the facts are because we love our children. To be sure, the validity of claims can be contested, as some parents have done with the diagnosis of attention deficit hyperactive disorder in their child and the prescription of the drug ritalin for that child. This, though, is a different matter entirely. It is one thing to question the uncritical application of a drug; it is quite another to roundly reject well-founded and long-established truths in the name of some quixotic ideal. Parental love does not support any

---

[6] I am enormously indebted here to J. David Velleman, "Love as a Moral Emotion," *Ethics* 109 (1999), although I do not accept his conclusions.

such approach to parenting. In this regard, I should like to suggest that just as we have the expression "misplaced compassion," we need something analogous when it comes to parental love. Compassion per se is a good thing. Yet, our compassion can be inappropriate. Parental love is never inappropriate. Yet, it can be very much misguided.

A consideration most relevant to our discussion is that love between adults differs in a fundamentally important way from love between parents and child. Adults bring to their interactions both an understanding and deep convictions with respect to how the conception of the right applies to them. They have a view of what counts as acceptable and unacceptable behavior on the part of others toward them. Or so it is when things proceed as they should, which may be less often than we would like to think. Still, the contrast with child-parent interaction is in principle a very sharp one, since under the best of circumstances no child could have a conception of the right in place – a conception of what counts as acceptable and unacceptable behavior toward it – at the outset of its life. With adults, one is warranted in at least presuming that they have a conception of the right as it applies to them, even if it turns out that this presumption must be rejected.[7] By contrast, one is not warranted in having this presumption with regard to children. On the contrary, the presumption goes

---

[7] Following the essay by Thomas Hill, Jr., "Servility and Self-Respect," one might say that self-respecting persons have a deep and abiding conception of the right as it applies to their lives, whereas the servile person does not. One can have very good reasons for thinking that a person is lacking in self-respect, e.g., a spouse who has been systematically battered over the years or an adult who was systematically neglected and abused throughout childhood. These are morally damaged individuals who, of course, are not to be discarded. However, moral theory has not attended to this issue as much as it ought. And I do not address the matter in this book.

the other way around, namely that children do not have such a conception of the right. Moreover, the facts never seem to warrant rejecting this latter presumption, no matter how gifted the child turns out to be. For not even a gifted child could have sufficient experience to understand and have deep convictions regarding a conception of the right.

It is first and foremost through interaction with its parents that the child acquires a conception of the right. When parents love a child in the manner that they should, the beginnings of the proper conception of the right are established in the child's life. This is the view presented in chapter 1, namely that the child has intrinsic moral value; accordingly, there are some things that no one is justified in doing to her or him. A child is not born knowing this precept or understanding its applications. Rather, it is through the words and deeds of the parents that the child acquires this precept and appreciates its implications. Thus, for example, the child comes to have respect for his own body because his parents show respect for his body. Typically, this form of respect happens in such a routine manner that it does not call attention to itself. But when this routine is violated, as in the case of child abuse, the damage to the child's sense of worth can be enormous. So while it may be routine for parents to allow a child to shower and use the bathroom facilities on his own after a certain age, there is nothing at all insignificant about doing so. It is only through the proper routine behavior with regard to such matters that the child acquires a deep sense of bodily propriety.

The issue of child abuse, which is naturally seen as abhorrent by decent folks, reveals in a rather stark way that the concept of the right comes into play at the very outset of the parent-child relationship, well before the child has a sense of self. Indeed, if parents waited until after the child's sense of self was in place before they respected his body, this would already be too late, because significant damage to the child's psychological well-being would already have occurred.

In general parents must respect their child if the child is to see himself not merely as an extension of his parents; and this entails something quite profound. For the child must witness, at least often enough, that his well-being suffices as a reason for his parents to refrain from doing things and, moreover, that they take delight in so behaving on his behalf. Parenting, then, can be as it should be only if the concept of the right is operative in the parent-child relationship and only if parents are delighted in following the right on behalf of their child and this is evident to the child. These considerations indicate that there is more plausibility than one might have thought to Rousseau's idea that the family is a model for society. Parents have enormous power over their child; and that power is appropriately regulated by a conception of the right. Indeed, the proper development of the child requires that this be so, even with parental love well in place. In society, the government has considerable power over each citizen; and that power is appropriately regulated by a conception of the right.

Because good parents naturally love their children, a conception of the right might seem otiose. After all, what loving parents would want to harm their child? None, presumably. But consider the difference between conveying to a child that something is good for her merely because one claims that it is, and conveying to that child that something is good for her because it is the right thing to do for her. Obviously, these two propositions do not have the same content. The first puts no restrictions at all on what one may say is good for the child; whereas the second clearly does. And love at its best cannot generate the second sentiment in the absence of a conception of the right. More to the point, the child cannot come to have an intrinsic sense of worth unless the child understands that it is because her parents love her that there are some things that they must do or refrain from doing because these things would enhance or diminish her well-being, as the case may be. Recall the idea in chapter 1 of an emotional imprimatur of self-valuing. The surest sign that persons value themselves is that they place limits on what others may do to them. It is from parents that children first learn that there are such limits.

3 FELLOW-FEELING AND A CONCEPTION OF THE RIGHT

Now, Rousseau observed that the absence of love stands as a most important difference between the parents of a family and the ruler of a society. For this reason, one might very well suppose that if a concept of the right is needed when love is present, then it follows all the more that a conception of the right is needed when it comes to regulating relations in the absence of love. Hence, the family underscores just how essential a concept of the right is to society. I shall not argue this point. Much of moral and political theory is about just this matter. What principles should govern a society has been much debated; hence, the contrasts and comparisons between, for example, justice as fairness, libertarianism, and utilitarianism. I do not have anything to add to this discussion. Rather, I wish to draw attention to another matter that is easily overlooked. Having argued that the family needs a concept of the right, I wish now to argue that society needs a parallel to parental love. It is in this regard that I find Rousseau's parallel between family and society remarkably fecund in a way that is often overlooked.

There is no gainsaying the importance of rights in society. But equal rights are not enough. In particular, equal rights are no substitute for general goodwill or fellow-feeling. The absence or presence of general goodwill is definitive of the moral climate of a society; and a moral climate informs the expectations that we can have of people regarding their genuine willingness to do what is right by others. Where general goodwill prevails, the members of society know that the citizens are willing to do right by others even if it is possible to wrong others with impunity. By contrast, with the absence of general goodwill in a society, the members of society know that by and large the citizens attach little or no importance to doing right by others for its own sake; so they are more than willing to set the precepts of society aside for the sake of their own advantage, however that might be defined.

General goodwill or fellow-feeling, then, is society's parallel to parental love. If sustained and constant parental love is taken out of the picture, this is essentially a disaster for the children, barring some type of formidable intervention. Similarly, if general goodwill is taken out of the picture, society crumbles. It does not matter what rights are articulated by a society's constitution or how eloquently they are articulated. If the members of a society are loath to abide by them, then that society will flounder mightily. When general goodwill is absent in a society, the most that can be expected of citizens generally is that they will adhere to the letter of the law. This is to say that there will be very little respect for the sanctity of the individual, which is the very raison d'etre of laws. In his important work *The Concept of Law*, H. L. A. Hart spoke of the internal point of view with respect to the law or a practice. The internal point of view is essentially the valuing of a norm or practice as worthy or appropriate. In England, citizens generally have the internal point of view regarding bowing before the Queen of England. People do so willingly as a show of respect. In society, general goodwill reflects the value that citizens in general place upon the political framework that is supportive of the flourishing of citizens. So while it is true that no single individual need have goodwill when it comes to the rights of citizens, it is manifestly false that general goodwill is unnecessary. For the complete absence of goodwill is chaos, as I shall establish momentarily.

I have just alluded to the difference between the macro and the micro levels of society. On any given day, at any given moment, precisely what we want is that our rights are respected; and if officers of the law are necessary in order accomplish that, then so be it. But when we move away from the specificity of the moment, what is of enormous importance is the fact that society supports bringing in officers of the law in order to ensure the protection of one's rights in the case at hand. Transitional phases in society make it particularly easy to miss the importance of general goodwill.

The Civil Rights Movement in the United States was a transitional phase during which, for example, the force of the law was sometimes employed in order to achieve integration in the country's educational institutions. At that point in time, it was fashionable for some members of society to embrace racist views in a very public manner. Recall the late Governor George Wallace who stood in front of a school entrance in defiant opposition to integration.[8] Nowadays, the very opposite is true. To be sure,

---

[8] For a discussion of Wallace, I am indebted to Dan T. Carter, *The Politics of Rage: George Wallace, the Origins of the New Conservatism, and the Transformation of American Politics* (New Orleans: Louisiana State University Press, 2000). One should also note his remarkable change of heart. I have discussed this in my essay "Forgiving the Unforgivable" in *Moral Philosophy and the Holocaust* (eds.)

there is still disagreement over what does or does not constitute racism and over what a commitment to racial equality entails, as the debate over affirmative action shows. Be that as it may, one would be hard pressed these days to find anyone who would embrace the segregation of yesteryear (setting aside individuals who belong to groups like the KKK). In other words, it is now the case that at the macro level society has become considerably more accepting of ethnic differences, which is to say that there is now general goodwill with regard to embracing ethnic and racial diversity in society. This is so even if, as some claim, racism still exists.

Anyone who thinks that there has not been much change at all in the society's general attitude regarding race and that the numerous changes in the law do not amount to much should contrast the public reaction to the lynching of blacks in the 1940s to the public reaction that would occur were a black lynched in this century. Then such horrors were greeted with little or no public outcry. Today, a wave of moral outrage would traverse the country. But suppose that this was not the case, and that a lynching today no more troubled the general public than it did more than sixty years ago, despite the considerable changes in the laws regarding race relations. So notwithstanding the fact that perpetrators of a lynching are apprehended, there is no public outcry whatsoever. There is no sense of righteous indignation throughout the country. Admittedly, this juxtaposition is somewhat difficult to imagine. The point, though, is that were this the

Eve Scarre and Geoffrey Scarre (Burlington, VT: Ashgate Press, 2003). For a searching discussion concerning the appropriate way to respond to evil, see Geoffrey Scarre, *After Evil: Responding to Wrong Doing* (Burlington, VT: Ashgate Press, 2004). See also Michele Moody-Adam, *op. cit.*, "Epilogue."

case, racial strife in the United States would be utterly explosive. For part of what contributes to racial harmony is not just that no one lynches, for example, but that when a lynching occurs, there is an outcry of righteous indignation throughout the land, and thus on the part of those who had nothing whatsoever to do with the act. In other words, what is needed is a general good-will or the fellow-feeling that underwrites and accords with the principle that lynching is unequivocally wrong. It is not merely that a society in which the citizens publicly deplore lynching is preferable to one in which the citizens do not (though persons guilty are apprehended and punished), it is that the latter society would be all but unbearable for those who are the object of lynching. This is because there would not be the desired and needed public affirmation that such an event is wrong. That is, the moral personhood of such individuals would not be receiving from the society the kind of affirmation that is appropriate regarding the wrongfulness of the behavior of lynching.[9] And this, quite simply, is an affront to the self-respect of such individuals.

In the absence of fellow-feeling, rights enforced are an affront to the self-respect of the citizens of a society. Persons are both getting and not getting what they deserve. On the one hand, they are getting the benefits to which they are entitled by virtue of their rights being enforced; on the other, though, they are not being affirmed as individuals who are deserving of those benefits. In the short run, obviously, we are more than willing to settle for the first without the second. In the long run, however, it is only the second that quenches our moral thirst, if you

---

[9] For the very felicitous expression, "moral personhood," which I employ at length in the following chapter, I am indebted to Richard Eldridge, *On Moral Personhood* (Chicago: University of Chicago, 1989).

will, because the second is a profound acknowledgement and affirmation of our moral personhood. We never outgrow the need for that affirmation.

Why is general goodwill so important? The answer is that it is the scaffolding upon which basic trust in society sits. Among reasonable people, wherever we have general goodwill, we have basic trust. This is the trust that a mere stranger in society willingly respects our rights. In the absence of general goodwill, it is no longer reasonable to believe that the citizens of our society have no interest in violating our rights; accordingly, in the absence of general goodwill, basic trust in the citizens of society is absolutely unwarranted. It must be understood that what we are most interested in is not that citizens are given their just punishment should they violate our rights, but that citizens do not, in the first place, have any wish to violate our rights even if they could do so with impunity. No sane person would be indifferent to the choice between, on the one hand, not being robbed at all and, on the other, being robbed but having one's assailant apprehended as well as being compensated for one's losses. The first option is rationally preferable, even when compensation is possible. As we know, though, it is not possible to compensate for some things. The loss of life comes readily to mind in this regard. This makes the first option all the more rationally preferable.

Now, if basic trust is absent throughout a society, then it follows that it is not rational for any member of society to expect that its citizens are generally inclined to act in accordance with the law if it is possible for them to get away with not doing so. Not only that, but it becomes irrational for any citizen to comply with the law if she or he cannot count on others to do likewise. The law itself, then, becomes a tyrant rather than a vehicle for facilitating cooperation between citizens and a conduit of mutual affirmation. Thus, in the absence of general goodwill in society, we are left with either chaos or totalitarianism, neither of which is desirable.

Much moral and political theory proceeds on the assumption that if we just get everyone to have the same rights, then everything in society will be just fine. What I think Rousseau understood better than most is that this assumption is plainly false, precisely because equality of rights in the absence of general goodwill is not a viable state of affairs. Radical social alienation is compatible with equal rights alone, because people are being required to do what they believe they should not have to do. This is why a shift in sentiment is so important when equality is being extended in novel ways. It is not enough that the beneficiaries of this extension believe that this is what they deserve. It is equally important that society in general comes to share that belief. Undeniably, violence is a way to bring about change. It is not, however, a way to sustain that change once it has been wrought. And it is this truth that is lost on so many. Lest there be any misunderstanding, the suggestion here is not that people should refrain from seeking change unless they have a way to sustain it. After all, evil is typically insufferable; and people rightly seek to overthrow it. The point, rather, is that advancing a new order that in turn is sustained by the people can prove to be a more formidable challenge than overthrowing evil itself.

This is why, to take a concrete example, Nelson Mandela was so crucial in South Africa's transition from apartheid to a democracy. His life's story, coupled with his majestic sense of moral timing, made it possible for blacks and whites alike to have the sense that a new order was indeed something that could be accomplished. A sense of hope and a spirit of willingness were his gifts to the transition that took place. Arguably, no one was better placed to do this. There can be little doubt that sheer chaos would have reigned had any black who had taken over the reins of the new South Africa declared that all blacks of the country shall now extract from whites all that is rightfully owed to blacks. Would such an approach have been justified on some level? Whatever the answer, the approach would have come at the expense of general goodwill across the entire population, the absence of which would have been disastrous for all. So the radical insistence upon rights misses two points: Rights do not amount to all that is needed, because general goodwill is absolutely necessary; over the long run, general goodwill serves us where rights often cannot.

This is also why the hyperbolic name-calling that has become characteristic of political disagreement is surely doing more harm than good. The most incontrovertible example of unvarnished evil in modern times is the Holocaust; and it has become fashionable to appropriate the terminology of the Holocaust in all sorts of inappropriate ways. So opponents of abortion refer to abortion as another holocaust, and advocates of gay marriages refer to those who oppose such marriages as Nazis. It is beyond the purview of this essay to take a stand on either issue; however, surely neither characterization is correct.

Most assuredly, the rhetorical force of "You are a Nazi" or "This practice is but another holocaust" is that the behavior in question has reached the very nadir of morally despicable behavior. The problem is that once this level of excoriation is employed, then all bets are off. The reason for this is very simple. If a person cannot be more evil in her or his behavior, then it does not much matter what else the person goes on to do. One's moral capital, as it were, has already been spent; for nothing is really gained in going on to say that a person's behavior is now even worse than that which the Nazis did. Not only is there nothing to gain, but also seeds of bitterness have been sown. And bitterness and goodwill are diametrically opposed: where one gains ground, the other necessarily loses ground. Thus, it follows that a society in which bitterness prevails is on a self-destructive course. This is so, though everyone should have an equal right to everything. Understandably, we typically associate equal rights with progress. What must not be overlooked is that we have progress here because general goodwill has followed in the wake of equal rights. This truth, however, is a contingent one. Accordingly, it is logically possible for there to be equal rights and in fact less progress, simply because bitterness comes to prevail instead of goodwill. Its absence gives rise to a deafening cacophony, thereby making reasonable discourse among citizens impossible. Thus, its absence is everyone's loss.

Now, just as motivation from duty simply cannot stand in for parental love, neither can motivation from duty stand in for fellow-feeling. Kant recognized the need for human beings to be valued. However, he tried to turn the valuing that is required here into a kind of cognitive perception of the other, along with the corresponding behavior that is appropriate to the moment. What the history of human relations shows, though, is that human beings desperately want more than this cognitive perception and its concomitant behavior.

Fellow-feeling is precisely the correct sentiment to invoke. This is because citizens, who are adults, are not subordinate to one another in their status as citizens; nor can it be supposed that they have the kinds of relations that would call forth the love of friendship. Only a very small society of people could all be friends, anyway. Of course, it must be acknowledged that the idea of a ruler such as Rousseau had in mind is out of the question. Besides, even he acknowledged that the ruler could not be motivated by love to do what is right by his or her citizens. I have invoked fellow-feeling because it very aptly captures the importance of the citizens of a society, both collectively and individually, wanting to do right by one another and wanting their society to be that kind of society; and this, in turn, is very much in keeping with the spirit of the social contract tradition. After all, if the people do not want to do right by one another, then it does not much matter anyway what a ruler wants or what the laws say.[10]

It is worth nothing that John Rawls and David Gauthier, both contract theorists, acknowledge that the stability of society is utterly impossible in the absence of something like the affective sentiment of fellow-feeling. Indeed, in his searching discussion of Rawls's *A Theory of Justice*, Brian Barry argues with considerable force that Rawls comes dangerously close to short-circuiting his formal argument for the principles of justice as fairness owing to the importance that he (Rawls) rightly attaches to social stability, which is inextricably tied to widespread fellow-feeling in society.[11] Recall John Rawls's majestic remarks in *A Theory of Justice*:[12]

> It is a feature of human sociability that we are by ourselves but parts of what we might be. We must look to others to attain the excellences that we must leave aside, or lack altogether.

[10] I borrow this point from H. L. A. Hart's *The Concept of Law* (Oxford: The Clarendon Press, 1961).

[11] *The Liberal Theory of Justice* (Oxford: Clarendon Press, 1973).

[12] (Harvard University Press, 1971), Section 79 "The Idea of Social Union." For an excellent discussion of Rawls in this regard, see Bertrand Guillarme, *Rawls et l'égalité démocratique* (Paris: Presses Universitaires de France, 1999), Part Two, and Susan Mendus, "The Importance of Love in Rawls's Theory of Justice," *The British Journal of Political Science* 29 (1999).

Rawls's suggestion here is that far from being threatened by the excellences exhibited by the members of society, the members of society take delight in one another's excellences. For one thing, if a person is excelling in the pursuit of the goals that, indeed, she or he chooses to pursue, then it would make no rational sense for that person to begrudge others their successes. For another, the different pursuits bring to the social collective a richness that most certainly could not be had otherwise. It is no doubt natural to think that the latter point holds only when individuals are pursuing different aims. Not so, however. Sports require the pursuit of the same goal by various people, as does singing in many instances. Choral singing is a case in point. No matter how mellifluous one person's voice might be, that single voice could never produce the tonality and harmony, and so the richness, of a 100-voice choir. Moreover, inspiration and encouragement often come from those who are most familiar with what we do rather than from those who have only a passing acquaintance with our pursuits. Rawls's sublime point, of course, is that one of the features of justice in society is that it generates a considerable measure of harmony among the citizens of that society – so much so that citizens take delight in one another's flourishing. There is another point that is perhaps less sublime but is no less important, namely that in the absence of such harmony a society cannot be a viable one.

As Barry noted, this line of argument is so very powerful that it seems decisive in and of itself: Between any two moral theories, the one to be preferred is the one that generates this kind of harmony among its citizens when implemented in the basic structure of society. Hence, Rawls's well-known argument from the original position seems unnecessary.

My aim here is not to assess the validity of Barry's claim with respect to Rawls's argument in *A Theory of Justice*. Rather, I am more interested in the fact that Rawls, himself, felt the need to draw attention to the importance of psychological stability, as achieved by fellow-feeling among the citizens of society. Likewise in the case of Gauthier. For Gauthier understood all too well that the very argument that made it rational for persons to accept certain moral restraints also made it rational for persons not to abide by those restraints if they could violate them without detection. He added the affective sentiments as a way of reining persons in.

The comparison between family and society is more apropos than one might be initially inclined to think. Typically, a family is no more than a collection of people with a certain degree of blood propinquity, usually mother, father, and children. Although strong ties of affection normally prevail between people thus related, this need not be so at all. It is common enough for men to abandon women whom they impregnate or to provide nothing more than child support. And women sometimes give their children up for adoption because they are not ready for the task of parenting. Some women who do this do not wish to have any further contact with the child to whom they give birth. Rarely, if ever, is this what anyone has in mind in speaking about family. Rather what comes to mind is a group of people – children and their parents – who are united by a bond of affection and who live together in considerable harmony. They also share in one another's fortunes and misfortunes, and so take delight in one another's successes and commiserate when one among them fails. This is certainly the ideal to which many initially aspire, even if many widely miss the mark. After all, the very idea of having a family would have next to no appeal were it not for the fact that the family is seen as holding out hope for such a bond of affection. At the level of society (the nation-state), it is possible for there to be widespread disgust among all the citizens of a society, with few, if any, seeing themselves as having anything in common with their fellow citizens. But likewise, this is not what normally comes to mind when we think of a society. Rather, we think of a set of shared, albeit loosely defined, values and tastes anchored by a sense of fellow-feeling. Just as the rich sense of family comes to more than blood propinquity, the rich sense of a society (nation-state) comes to more than merely a collection of persons with the same citizenship primarily occupying a well-defined geographical space. With the rich sense of family, bonds of affection are a sine qua non. With the rich sense of society, fellow-feeling is a sine qua non.

4   Love and Fellow-Feeling Are Not Zero-Sum

I turn now to another important parallel between the family and society, which is that neither parental love nor fellow-feeling is a zero-sum good. This is of great significance because of the affirmation that both provide. In the simplest of terms, we have a zero-sum situation when one person's gain of a certain amount entails that at least one other person must lose out on that very same amount. For instance, a bigger slice of the pie for one person necessarily entails that there is less pie left for others. Conversely, if the person takes less pie than intended, then necessarily others have more. The formal presupposition of a zero-sum situation is a fixed and nonreplenishable good.

A truly marvelous fact about parental love is that it is not in any way a zero-sum good. Parental love for one child does not entail less parental love for another child. This is because love is not in any way depleted by its expression. There is not even the need to recover from the expression of love for a child before one can move on to the next child. Hence, showing love to one child does not mean that there is less love or that a child must wait for parental love to replenish itself. Each child can be loved most richly and equally so, and at any given time. Accordingly, one of the most remarkable and seminal lessons that a child learns is that there is not in any way less love for her or him, given a manifest display of love for other siblings.

Rousseau held that a just society is one in which all citizens could feel equally protected and, most importantly, equally supported by the government of their society. There simply could not be a better precursor of this political ideal than a family situation in which it is true that all siblings are richly and equally loved by their parents and, moreover, all siblings have the conviction that this so. Although the idea of equality may have its most eloquent articulation in the words of political theorists, its most profound and eloquent experience is in the family. The most visceral feelings of equality are secured in the family. The idea that parental love can be perceived by all the children of a family as a good that is not zero-sum is especially noteworthy when one considers both that the manifestation of parental love simply cannot be understood in terms of a set of well-defined acts, and that children have different needs in this regard. Naturally, there are some things that are absolutely incompatible with being a good parent. In truth, the list of things here may be longer than we want to acknowledge, because children are so in need of their parents. However, even with the list of things well established, countless is the number of ways in which parental love may be properly and effectively expressed. A kiss, or a hug, or a smile, or merely standing over a child with a look of adoration can all count as displays of affection. A mere wink from a parent can sometimes mean everything to a child. What is more, children will often differ in their preferred way of being the object of their parents' affection, which brings us to a very important point.

The reality that parental love is not a zero-sum good serves as an important psychological bridge, if you will, for a most important aspect of parenting, namely that differences in the ways in which parents treat each child are roundly and fully compatible with parents equally affirming their love for their children. The reality that parental love is not zero-sum serves as a psychological bridge because if each child knows that she or he is as much the object of parental love as any other child, and each child is being fully loved, then the manner in which each child is loved is of no consequence to the others. Surely, one aspect of the majesty of parental love is that when such love is as it ought to be, then the children experience the reality of both truths: the truth that parental love is not depletable by its expression; and, the truth that differences in the expression of parental love, in the absence of untoward considerations, are roundly compatible with parents loving all of their children equally and fully.

As an aside, the thesis that parental love cannot be depleted by its expression should not be confused with the very different thesis that parental love can never cease to obtain. The nature of love is such that no fact or truth makes it conceptually impossible to continue loving a person. There is no conceptual blunder involved if the parents of a serial killer, for instance, continue to love their child. They could continue to do so, even as they understand that he is going to prison and, in fact, approve of this. Love, as I noted earlier, is not incompatible with punishment. On the other hand, love for another can so wane that it ceases to be there at all. No doubt romantic love readily comes to mind as an example. However, this can happen between any two people regardless of their biological ties or lack thereof. Family members can, in truth, come to despise one another.

As was noted earlier, children will often differ in their preferred way of being the object of their parents' affection, which brings us to another important point. An affectionate tickle may mean everything to one child, whereas the other detests this. One child wants lots of very explicit encouragement, the other just wants to know that her parents are there should anything go wrong. Or, from a rather different direction, the criticism of one child may have to be very circumspect, whereas the other can handle a direct criticism as long as it is accompanied by a hug. And so on. As I have just said: Countless are the ways in which parental love can be effectively and properly expressed. Not only are there differences from one child to the next, but also the very same child may prefer or need some forms of affection in some instances and other forms in other instances. The successful completion of the rites of a religious confirmation undoubtedly call for parental love to express itself rather differently from what is appropriate to a child's winning the national spelling contest for thirteen-year-olds. Good parents are mindful of this.

Nonetheless, parental love can be equal, and perceived as equal by all the children of the family, without there necessarily being one particular thing that the parents do equally with regard to all of their children. Not even basic needs have to be addressed in exactly the same way for each child. Health, dietary, and clothing needs may all be different from one child to the next. Shelter, because it is typically the same house for all family members, perhaps comes the closest to being precisely the same for all, though we can have important differences here as well, because health needs may require a particular configuration with regard to shelter. A child with severe asthma, for instance, may need to have a room with certain equipment in it. If anything is clear, then, it is that parental love at its very best is compatible with a wealth of differences among the children of the family. Parents can, of course, commit the awful mistake of favoring one child over another. For our purposes, though, the very substantive point is that there is nothing about parental love as such, nor its variety of expression, that lends itself to parents favoring one child over another. In particular, differences between children are not thereby a catalyst for parents favoring one child over another.

The family shows in a most dramatic way that all children can be affirmed equally, in terms of parental love, without that very affirmation being identical in its form. Indeed, equality with respect to the latter would be disastrous. The parallel in society, of course, would be that fellow-feeling is also not a zero-sum good. Expressions of fellow-felling for one citizen or one group of citizens does not mean that there is less fellow-feeling for the others. Thus, just as it would be a mistake to treat all children in exactly the same way in order to show them all that they are equally loved, it would be a mistake to treat all citizens in exactly the same way in order to secure on the part of each the conviction that her or his standing in society as a citizen is equal to the standing of all other citizens. Children have different needs and interests. And they often flourish in very different ways. Needless to say, the exact same thing can be said about the citizens of society.

At first glance, one might think that the parallel simply does not hold. But I imagine that Rousseau must have reasoned as follows: The aim of parenting (when this is as it should be) is that each of the children flourishes. Parenting can have no other legitimate aim. Likewise, the aim of society is that each of its citizens flourishes. Society can have no other legitimate aim. In being committed to the flourishing of their children, good parents do not hold that all their children have the same abilities, talents, and interests. That would be detrimental. Yet, these differences notwithstanding, good parents are committed to the flourishing of each child in the ways that the child's abilities will allow. Good parenting does not ignore important differences in the name of equality. The same holds for society. The language of the great constitutions of modern time holds that all persons are equal as human beings. The claim is not, however, that all persons have the same abilities, talents, and interests. A good society, then, does not ignore these differences in the name of some fixed grid, but offers instead the possibility of flourishing across the vast differences that are characteristic of the human race. With parenting, it would be utterly inappropriate for the parents to have as their aim that each of the children be exactly alike and so to distribute the resources of the family accordingly. The same holds for the society.

Imagine a family with three children. One of them, call her Rachelie, is absolutely gifted. Although the other two obviously have considerable talent, they cannot be called gifted. Rachelie, by contrast, calls to mind John Stuart Mill. At the age of seven, she reads at the college level; she already understands calculus and trigonometry; and she is well on her way to mastering Latin. Now, imagine her parents arguing that fair is fair. What is good for one child is good for all the others; accordingly, we must treat Rachelie exactly like we treat the other two notwithstanding the fact that we realize that this means that she will not even come close to developing to her full potential. After all, so they continue, we love them all equally. Needless to say, this would be abominable. The very thought that parental love and fairness require such a thing is just so much nonsense. Allowing Rachelie to languish would be proof that they did not love them all equally, since loving Rachelie as much as the other two are loved would entail seeing to it that her gifts are realized, which does not in the least entail showing her more love.

We can make the same point from the opposite direction. Suppose that instead of being marvelously gifted it turns out that Rachelie suffers from severe mental retardation. She needs far more attention than the other two children need. It would be despicable not to give her this extra attention on the grounds that this would not be fair to the others. Or, it would be just as despicable to treat the other two in the way that Rachelie is treated, since that would be inimical to their flourishing. Yet again, the parents love them all equally.

It is certainly possible that differences in the treatment of children could result in differences in affirmation. It is hardly a conceptual truth, however, that things must turn out that way. Good parenting would be absolutely impossible if that were the case. Lots of attention and care are required in order make sure that differences in treatment do not turn into differences in affirmation. Ironically, this is far from being a very weighty consideration against different forms of treatment as appropriate to each child. This is because an inexorable commitment to sameness of treatment is an absolute guarantee that one or more children will be harmed.

Now, the claim that parental love is not a zero-sum phenomenon must not be confused with the quite different and obviously false claim that family resources are not a zero-sum phenomenon. Moreover, it is clear that generally speaking greater resources permit parents to do more for their children. With limited financial resources there can be severe restraints on what parents can do for their children. In fact, resources can be over-taxed, requiring parents to make tough, and quite uncomfortable, decisions. This might be the case if, for example, one child has a debilitating illness or there are twins whose many demanding needs come at precisely the same time. Yet, taxed resources are compatible with all the children having the unshakable conviction that their parents are committed to doing the best they can under the circumstances to ensure their flourishing; and it is precisely this conviction that is secured on the part of each child when parental love is as it should be. Although resources are indeed a zero-sum good, a most significant truth is that resources, however limited they might be, do not turn parental love into a zero-sum good. People with essentially no resources at all to call their own, namely those who are enslaved, may nonetheless find a way to love all of their children equally.

Let us now turn to society. Given the claim that fellow-feeling is society's analogue to parental love, the first thing to note is that, like love, fellow-feeling is not diminished by its expression. Expressing fellow-feeling for some members of society does not leave less to be expressed for others in the society. Nor need the expression of fellow-feeling take the same form across every member of society. And just as limited resources in the family do not turn parental love into a zero-sum good, it is also the case that limited resources in society do not turn fellow-feeling into a zero-sum good. During the Great Depression, the resources in society were extremely limited. Yet, it appears that fellow-feeling ran especially high.

While I shall not take up the topic of multiculturalism, as such, it is worth noting that multiculturalism essentially embodies the view that in order to affirm all members of society, it is not at all the case that society need treat everyone exactly alike in all respects. Multiculturalism takes seriously the differences in society between individuals on the grounds that culture is a fundamental aspect of a person's identity. Treating everyone exactly alike in all respects is deemed to be incompatible with respecting different cultures. Thus, according to multiculturalism, it is not treating everyone exactly alike that affirms all the members of society-at-large, but treating the different members of society in accordance with the demands of their cultural identity that affirms the members of society-at-large. Lesbians and gays insist that there is an identity, a place apart from heterosexual culture, that corresponds to these categories, and that a just society contributes to the flourishing of one as much as it contributes to the other. Now, my earlier remarks regarding fellow-feeling apply with equal force to the concerns of multiculturalists. The idea is not simply that different cultural groups should be left to their own devices. Rather, there should be mutual respect among and for all cultural groups.

What is ironic in all of this is that the one difference that many wish to discount is the difference that is typically the most sure and identifiable at the biological level, namely the difference between female and male. One naturally wonders how can it be that the differences between Arabs and Latinos or homosexuals and heterosexuals be of such great significance, but not the differences between women and men, since this latter difference vividly manifests amid all the other differences and not the other way around? It cannot be that the difference between women and men is trivial. Indeed, it certainly is not trivial to lesbians and gays. Still, the most vivid and immutable difference in human nature seems to be the one that many members of contemporary society would find unacceptable from the standpoint of the Rousseauian idea of different treatment but equal affirmation. Yet the hardest case underscores the point.

Whatever else is true, women in general are capable of bearing children, and a great many chose to do so. Men, by contrast, are biologically incapable of doing so. It is not clear how a society could be a just society if it did not take into account this difference between women and men in the arrangement of its institutions. Taking this difference into account would not entail relegating women to a higher or lower status than men on any social, political, or moral plane. But it most certainly would entail that women and men should be treated differently when a woman is pregnant. And if one considers that a woman puts her life at risk to some extent in bringing a child into this world, then there is a moral attitude that is appropriate to this reality for which there is no obvious parallel with regard to the male. The matter of health generally underscores the importance of taking seriously the differences between women and men. With the passing of time, breast cancer becomes a concern for women, whereas prostate cancer becomes a concern for men. A social and political reality that acknowledges this, far from undermining equality of citizenship, mightily affirms it.

A different and somewhat more complicated example is as follows. It is a fact that both women and men can be raped; and in either case, this is a most horrendous wrong to experience. That said, there is a difference of fundamental importance between the two cases. However small the probability, rape of a woman can give rise to pregnancy. Even if abortion is an option, that hardly detracts from the angst that a woman will have. For there is nothing intrinsically pleasant about the experience of having an abortion. Men, on the other hand, do not have this worry, regardless of the other concerns that they may have. What follows from this difference? It does not follow, certainly, that women should stay home or wear chastity belts or do some other ridiculous thing in order to ensure that they are not raped. Just so, any society that is unmindful of this difference between women and men with regard to this wrong would be an extremely negligent one. If nothing else, officials handling rape offenses need to be sensitive to this difference. Ordinary citizens need to be sensitive to this difference as well. Thus, when a man sees a female rape victim in a corner, it should be sensibilities to the concerns of women, and not prudishness, that incline him to get his wife to assist the victim. Surprisingly, if instead the rape victim is a man, it is not automatically a settled matter that assistance from a man is immediately preferable, since maleness is nonetheless symbolic of the individual who perpetrated the wrong.

Now if the way in which people experience the world is constitutive of their identity, as many multiculturalists would say, then an inexorable sameness of treatment has to be a mistake. This truth does not cease to be valid when it comes to women and men. The problem is not in acknowledging substantive differences where they exist. Rather, it is in either attributing differences to people that have no basis whatsoever in reality, or in drawing tendentious conclusions with regard to these differences. This is so whether we are talking about the differences between one ethnic group and another or the differences between women and men. In a just society neither kind of error is committed. In the past, people have often used differences between groups as a basis for discrimination, something that we wish to avoid. But the end of discrimination lies not in treating everyone exactly the same in all respects, but in underwriting the flourishing of everyone in accordance with bonafide differences. It is this truth that is at the very heart of Rousseau's *Social Contract*. In a just society, citizens aim to articulate differences with fairness, clarity, and purity of heart. Everyone is guided by the truth that it is as much a mistake to deny differences that are real as it is to manufacture differences for the sake of personal gain. Although none of this is easy, fellow-feeling makes the process virtuous rather than vicious.

When fellow-feeling is as it should be, then society is committed to all of its members flourishing or being excellent in accordance with their abilities and preferences, as constrained by the resources available. This is not to say, however, that each person should exhibit the same level of excellence. When fellow-feeling is as it should be, the problem is not that others exhibit a level of excellence that we do not exhibit, but that others do so because they were given an unfair advantage over us. And here, the family is ever so illuminating. Recall the example of Rachelie, the prodigy. No sibling can rightly complain simply on the grounds that he is not as gifted as Rachelie is. A sibling would have grounds for complaint only if he had reason to believe that his parents had stunted his intellectual growth or that they were not committed to his flourishing to the extent that his abilities permitted. The latter, of course, would mean that parents did not have the love for him that they should have had. When parents rightly handle a significant differential in talent between their children, there is no lack of love between the siblings at all. Quite the contrary, there is often a strong bond of appreciation between them. This is because the equal parental love for all ensures that all appreciate and respect the good that the others do, with no exception being made for the gifted one.

At the level of society, fellow-feeling should operate in precisely the same way. We can appreciate the genius of an Einstein or a Hawking. But, alas, one can contribute most significantly to the good of society without having the intellectual power of either of these two individuals. And when fellow-feeling in a society is as it should be, the good that everyone does is appreciated. On the one hand, it would be foolish to pretend that all could reach the excellence of an Einstein or a Hawking and just as foolish and wrong to hold back those who can. On the other, it would be just as foolish and wrong to discount the innumerable ways that people contribute to the good of society without having the talent of a genius within their reach.

Countless are the ways in which parents can affirm their children, regardless of the level of intellectual talent that each child possesses. So it is in a society in which fellow-feeling abounds. In either case, the only real restraint is that the affirmation must be genuine. When affirmation is genuine it is savored; and in being savored it invigorates. By contrast, when affirmation is disingenuous, it rings hollow in due course. Instead of being left with a beautiful memory that reaffirms one again and again, one is left trying to breathe life into the so-called words of praise. One is left trying to find emotional resonance where none exists. One is typically left longing for the very affirmation that one had supposedly received. This is because with disingenuous affirmation the sincerity never quite has the uptake that it is supposed to have. For sincerity is necessarily affective in character. Although two people can utter the very same words of praise, we can feel quite moved by the one and quite mocked by the other, all owing to the depth of sincerity present in one case and painfully absent in the other. The point holds whether we are talking about affirmation from parents or fellow citizens. The affectivity is tied to the emotional significance that we attach to the hearer believing that we uttered the words because they are true and express our genuine intent, and to the hearer believing that we wanted her or him to hear what we said. This explains why accidental sincerity makes no sense. It also explains why calling into question our sincerity typically occasions anger on our part. Alas, doing so is often viewed as an affront to our integrity.

I should conclude this section with a brief word about rankings and excellence. In the ideal world, there would be a direct correlation between attaining the number one ranking and exhibiting superior excellence. In the actual world, however, there is very often a conspicuous lack of excellence on the part of those who have attained the number one ranking. This is because it has come to pass that mere indicators that something might be excellent in some form or other have been elevated to the status of demonstrative proof of the excellence in question. For example, the number of copies that a book has sold is certainly an indicator that the book may be an excellent one. But it simply does not follow that book A surpasses book B in excellence simply because more copies of book A have been sold. The very idea of excellence becomes perverted if, as a matter of course, the excellence is equated to quantitative outcomes, such as the number of copies that have been sold. And one reason for this is that quantitative outcomes, as such, are easily enough manipulated in order to achieve the desired result. Mel Gibson's *The Passion of the Christ* is a wonderful illustration of this point, precisely because there are two interesting ways to grasp its success – although the charitable interpretation seems to be the more plausible explanation for the film's success.

To begin with, it is noteworthy that for the initial five-day period, there are only two other films that earned more than Gibson's film, namely *Matrix Reloaded* and *Spider-Man*. Surprisingly, for the same time period, his film even did better than *Lord of the Rings*. *Forbes* predicted that the film would gross around

$600 million. On the one hand, it could be said that religious fundamentalists merely wanted to ensure the success of the film; hence, they purchased tickets for the film in large blocks. On this interpretation, what motivated people to see the film is simply the fact that they could do so for free. On the other hand, it could be said that religious fundamentalists found the film to be an extraordinary portrayal of the story of the death of Christ; and because they wanted others to share in this moment, they purchased tickets in large blocks. On this interpretation, what motivated people to see the film is the fact that they, too, wanted to have the extraordinary religious experience that viewing the film was said to occasion. In any case, notwithstanding the film's astounding economic success, precisely what seems to have been an issue is the quality of the film. And that would be rather uninteresting but for the fact that Hollywood has been all too quick to associate the economic success of a film with its being excellent in some way or other. However, all sorts of people roundly denounced Gibson's film, because it was either anti-Semitic or gratuitously violent.[13]

Whether one agrees with the critics or not – indeed, whether or not the critics themselves adequately grasped the significance of their stance – it illustrates that there is in fact a profound difference between an activity or work achieving the rank of #1 by

---

[13] As to the charge of gratuitous violence, it seems to me that an editorial in *Le Monde*, entitled "L'affaire Mel Gibson ou les deux faces du christianisme" (April 1, 2004) got it just right: "L'œuvre de Mel Gibson trempe dans la violence du temps du Christ comme dans celle du monde d'aujourd'hui. Une violence charnelle, indicible qui n'est pas, pour le réalisateur, un acte gratuit, une mise en scène d'épouvante pour faire hurler les foules et payer le chaland, mais un mode d'expression pédagogique pour faire accéder le spectateur au mystère de la crucifixion, à la mort du Christ pour la rédemption de tous les hommes."

economic success, and reaching the top by exhibiting superior excellence. When criteria like the economic success of a work become definitive of excellence, then the very idea of excellence has been eviscerated. And in a society that eviscerates the very idea of excellence, flourishing becomes an empty notion. In this regard, the family stands once more as a model for society. It would be unthinkable for loving parents to define the excellences exhibited by their children in terms of a purely quantitative vector like economic success. Needless to say, it would be impossible for parents who so behaved to bestow upon their children a sense of uniqueness without invidious comparison. Hence, the equal affirmation of all children could not be achieved. In a society that privileges economic success above all, it is similarly the case that the equal affirmation of all citizens is not possible. There would be a profound discord between the language of equality for all and the social reality that informed each person's lived experiences.

5   SELF-COMMAND

I turn now to a very different kind of consideration whereby the family serves as a model for the state, namely that the family brings out the truth that proper development of the self is not rightly construed simply in terms of the satisfaction of desires. This is to be understood in at least two ways: (1) not every self-regarding want that a person has is to be satisfied and (2) there are things that one must do even if one does not want to do them. Parents who raised a child to believe that all self-regarding wants should be satisfied or that one may do only what one wants to do would most certainly have failed to raise their child properly, at least given the world as we know it, where children often have a plethora of wants that are unacceptable on a variety of accounts.

Sometimes the unacceptable wants reflect an inappropriate attitude on the part of the child, as when a child wishes to take more
than her or his share; sometimes it is owing to the child's not having accurate information, as when the child mistakes medicine
for candy. In any case, surely one of the ways in which the child
learns both (1) and (2) above is by observing the parents. They
do not satisfy all of their self-regarding wants; and sometimes
they do what they do not wish to do. Parents who do without for
the sake of their children exemplify the first point; and parents
who act on behalf of their children in spite of illness or profound tiredness illustrate the second one. Likewise for parents
who forgo significant opportunities for the sake of the well-being
of their children. After all, having an extremely well-paying job
does not necessarily make for being a good parent, since parenting in absentia is not parenting at all. Parents who satisfied all of
their self-regarding wants or who did only what they wanted to
do could not possibly be good parents. The exception, of course,
would be the highly unlikely case in which satisfying all of their
self-regarding wants turned out to be unquestionably beneficial
for the child. In reality, the actual wants and feelings of parents
may, from time to time, be dramatically at odds with what is good
for both the family and the child. Needless to say, it is also relevant that as wife and husband, parents should exemplify points
(1) and (2) in their own interactions, because in so doing they
serve as very influential role models for their child. A child could
not want for a better role model in this regard than witnessing
her or his own parents setting aside their own interests from time
to time for both one another's sake and the child's sake.

In witnessing self-command on the part of her or his parents,
the child learns that the propriety of this virtue in life is not tied
to an individual's being subordinate to someone. For parents are

not subordinate to one another; nor *a fortiori* are they subordinate to the child. This reality underscores the fact that in the family self-command springs from the sentiment of love. What is more, this is how the child experiences the display of self-command on the part of her or his parents.

Now, it is tempting to think that not satisfying all wants of family members is necessarily linked to limited resources. But this would be a mistake, because it is false that where a family has unlimited resources, then all wants should be satisfied. Familial love is incompatible with each person simply satisfying her or his own wants, even if the family has unlimited resources. This is a conceptual point that follows from the very idea of love. We can see this without making the futile attempt of trying to define love. Whatever else is true, to love another is to accord that person's life weight in one's own life that is independent of one's wants. And no such weight is accorded if one's own wants always take precedence over that person's life. More precisely, one cannot – whatever one's own station in life; whatever the other's – convey the sentiment of love toward an individual if one insists that the person must always subordinate her or his wants to one's wants. The point here is not that we have true love only if we have love between equals. That is surely false, since parents and children are not equals. Nor, quite interestingly, does it follow from what has been said that true love can occur only in a just relationship. Or so it is, given the truth that there are many ways in which a relationship can be unjust. For even a sexist marital relationship that does entail some subordination on the part of woman to man does not entail that every want the wife has must be subordinate to the wants of her husband. A similar point holds for love relationships in the context of slavery.

The point that love cannot entail the complete subordination of another individual to one's own wants enables us to distinguish sharply between a relationship of love and one of utter servility. In an utterly servile relationship, the other's life has no weight independently of one's own wants, no matter how much the other does for one; no matter how willingly the person does it. Herein lies part of the instability of servility. No self-respecting person can continuously give to another without supposing that she or he is owed some gratitude. However, a person who believes that she is owed some gratitude is one who believes she should be accorded a certain weight that is independent of the other's wants.

A most interesting observation to be gleaned from the preceding remarks is that love and the virtue of self-command are inextricably linked. Having the virtue of self-command is a consequence of according independent weight to the life of a loved-one, and so conducting oneself. If part of what is involved in loving another is, by both word and deed, making it clear to that person from time to time that her or his concerns are more important than the satisfaction of our own wants, then we must regulate ourselves accordingly. Mutual love between two people does not alter this. Indeed, the paradoxes of altruism are well known.[14] Each member of a group of people can be so busy trying to please one another that the group ends up doing what no one in fact really wants to do. A group of thoroughgoing

---

[14] For a discussion of these problems, see Richmond Campbell and Lanning Sowden (eds.), *The Paradoxes of Rationality and Cooperation: Prisoner's Dilemma and Newcomb's Problem* (Vancouver: The University of British Columbia Press, 1985). See also Jean-Pierre Dupuy, "Les Paradoxes du Raisonnement Rétrograde," in Jean-Pierre Dupuy and Pierre Livet (eds.), *Les limites de la rationalité* (Paris: Éditions La Découverte, 1997).

altruists would, as a matter of fact, actually have to work at pleasing one another, because such a group of individuals could not simply act on the impulse to comply with the articulated wishes of one another. This impulse would have to be resisted in favor of endeavoring to understand what might be wanted by, among other things, looking at shared histories. Self-command in the form of self-restraint would be essential, although the self-restraint would take a different form.

Now, from the standpoint of the family, the inextricable link between love and self-command is of great importance. In the absence of unusual circumstances, we do not normally think of the family as being the context for this virtue to find its richest expression, supposing instead that war or a den of iniquity best showcases this virtue. Yet, the family is just such a context, owing to its link to love. The virtue of self-command is essential to wholesome interaction between wife and husband, on the one hand, and parent and child, on the other. Indeed, if it is true that the child naturally loves the parents from very early on, part of the child's development includes the acquisition of self-command in expressing love toward her or his parents. Both a three-year-old and a thirteen-year-old may want to express affection to a parent. However, it is only the latter who is very much guided by a sense of whether or not it is appropriate to do this under the circumstances. Or, both a three-year-old and a thirteen-year-old may want something from a parent. Once more, though, it is the latter who is expected to understand and accept the fact that he or she may have to forgo the item because the house was just destroyed in a fire or because the other parent has just taken extremely ill. Insofar as the thirteen-year-old exhibits the appropriate behavior in each situation, he or she displays a level of self-command.

Quite relevant here is W. D. Falk's lovely distinction between goading and guiding.[15] Goading involves force or threat of force; guiding involves giving reasons. As with animals, an infant is essentially goaded along; whereas we reason, up to a point at any rate, with a thirteen-year-old. One does not really give an infant a reason why it should move out of harm's way, one simply swoops it out of harm's way, which is precisely what animals do on behalf of their young. Human beings possess the ability to speak a language, which allows for the possibility of commands. Thus, one may say to an infant: Stop! Don't do that! Reasons may be proffered; however, what is efficacious in these instances is simply the command. The virtue of self-command presupposes that an individual will accord reasons their proper weight and, on that account alone, will behave accordingly. Giving an infant reasons why it cannot have or do something is generally to no avail; whereas with a thirteen-year-old, one expects in many instances that the appropriate reasons will suffice as an explanation for why the teenager cannot have or do something. Recalling our example in the preceding paragraph, a three-year-old simply cannot be expected to attach the appropriate weight to the reason (for not getting what he wants) that the house was destroyed by fire or that the other parent suddenly took extremely ill. By contrast, a thirteen-year-old can. All the more so, then, one expects reasons to function in this way in the life of adults. For as I have already indicated just a few paragraphs ago, self-command begins with the adults of the family.

[15] See "Goading and Guiding," in his collected papers, *Ought, Reason, and Morality* (Ithaca, NY: Cornell University Press, 1986). It is significant from a moral point of view that animals are not guided (that is, reasoned with) by their parents, but are only goaded.

I have argued that love and self-command are inextricably linked. As one might imagine, in moving from the family to society, a like claim can be made for fellow-feeling and the virtue of self-command. A just society is not simply one in which people do no kill or rob or rape one another. It is one in which people do not do these things of their own accord, because they see themselves as having reasons of the appropriate kind to refrain from engaging in such behavior. This point can be understood on two levels. One is that a person's moral character is such that she or he is not disposed – nay, not even tempted – so to behave; and they reinforce that character. The other is that a person will take the appropriate steps to prevent herself from so behaving if she should have any reason to believe that circumstances would result in her doing the wrong that she does not want to do. In a word, fellow-feeling expresses itself in the desire to do right by others and the willingness to take the necessary steps to ensure that one will so behave should one have any reason to think that one will miss the mark.

The story of Ulysses and the sirens, in Greek mythology, is no doubt a drastic illustration of self-command, where one does the right thing even if this means having oneself restrained in the present so that one will not succumb to the undesirable in the future. Most of us in life will never have to face resisting something so powerful as the sirens that Ulysses faced.[16] Nonetheless, the opportunity to exhibit self-command presents itself in very mundane contexts. The most well known of these is the self-command necessary to make sure that one does not drive while under the influence of alcohol. Another instance, from a very

---

[16] For an excellent discussion of Ulysses's actions from a game theoretic action, see Edward McClennen, "*Rationalité et règles,*" in Dupuy et Livet, *op. cit.*

different direction, would be keeping one's sidewalk clean during inclement weather. Self-command is an excellence the possession of which by the members of society makes a profound difference to the moral climate of society. Insofar as it is possible for the people of a society to have a sense of unity, it is necessary that the virtue of self-command is widely exercised. I shall illustrate this more fully in the following chapter.

4

From Family to *E Pluribus Unum*

In Rousseau's *Social Contract*, we find one the most moving passages in the social contract tradition ever written. It reads as follows:

> Whatever advantages man is deprived of in the State of Nature, he fully regains in Civil Society. His faculties are engaged and fully developed, his ideas are broadened, and his sentiments are ennobled. Indeed, his very soul is entirely elevated.

> Man should continuously bless that wonderful moment when he was uprooted forever from the state of being a stupid and limited animal in the State of Nature, and made an intelligent being and a man in Civil Society.

Philosophical writing does not wax more rhapsodic than this. If these remarks describe what Civil Society affords each and every one of its members, nothing could be more rational for a person than to want to be a member of Civil Society. Yet, a note of caution must be sounded. For although this passage certainly implies that every member of society is better off, the idea does not seem to be that this is because society is the best conduit for the maximization of the self-interests of each person insofar as humans beings must live together. More precisely, the idea does not seem to be that Civil Society is preferable because it affords individuals in abundance whatever it is that they might have very much wanted to have in the State of Nature. Quite the contrary, the thought conveyed by this passage is that Civil Society gives rise to such an extraordinary transformation on the part of human beings by virtue of which they are all better off that the individual of Civil Society is a different kind of being altogether from the individual of the State of Nature. Accordingly, a linear maximization model would miss the mark in terms of explicating why persons are better off in Civil Society.

1 Beyond Self-Interest

Needless to say, Rousseau did not fail to recognize that society advances the self-interests of human beings. Nor did he fail to think that initially people came together out of self-interested reasons. What he rejected, though, is the view that it is only the promotion of everyone's self-interests that serves as the glue that holds society together. So although self-interest served as a catalyst in the formation of society, self-interest is not the motivational engine, if you will, by virtue of which society remains intact. This is because Rousseau held that in a just society a wealth of affective sentiments became the motivational engine instead.

A simple example might be instructive. Imagine the case of Aaron and Opidopo, who find themselves working together for Natasha Nacherie. Although there is no hostility between them, they would not have otherwise interacted, but for the fact that they were both in need of work; and they need to cooperate in order to remain secure in their job. Accordingly, it is only for self-interested reasons that they begin cooperating with one another.

They soon discover, however, not only that they work well together, but also that they actually enjoy working with one another. They take delight in one another's company and both find that their own lives are wondrously enriched through interacting with one another. They actually become friends – the best of friends. As best friends, there is now a remarkable cooperation between Aaron and Opidopo, so much so that they would now make a point of working together. Needless to say, the motivational structure of their cooperation has changed from self-interest, which initially occasioned their interaction, to friendship and goodwill. So although it is as true now as it has always been that they need to cooperate in order to maintain their job and, moreover, there has been cooperation between them from the very start, it is false that the motivational character of their cooperation is the same now as it was at the outset. For the motivational structure of friendship is not that of self-interest. Yet, it is true nonetheless that in the absence of cooperation between them they cannot do their job well. Worse, neither would have a job. This example shows that as a purely conceptual matter it is fallacious reasoning to hold that the motivation that gave rise to a kind of interaction and the motivation that sustains that interaction must be one and the same. The self-interested person seeks to advance her or his interest wherever that is possible and would do so at any time were it possible so to behave with impunity.

So Rousseau, or any contract theorist, could consistently hold that although self-interested concerns generated the formation of society, self-interested concerns do not sustain society. The passages from Rousseau quoted at the outset are, I suggest, best understood as reflecting Rousseau's view that the richness of society sustains itself independent of the self-interested reasons that first prompted human beings to come together and form a society. This is owing to the transformation that occurs in human beings on account of their being a part of society, because the affective sentiments are awakened. It need not be thought that self-interest evaporates, but only that it is not the primary motivation that sustains society. After all, it is rare that any human being acts with a single motivation. Just so, the existence of more than one motivation for an individual's behavior is compatible with there being one that was and is sufficient to motivate the person to behave as she or he does. What is more, one can have a self-interested reason for acting and not be motivated by it. That it is in a husband's self-interest to give his wife flowers for Valentine's Day does not entail that he is moved by self-interest so to behave.

From the standpoint of rational choice theory, this thinking on Rousseau's part is quite serendipitous. On the one hand, any attempt to give a purely self-interested argument (not just for the formation of society, but) for the continued existence of society encounters, as is well known, an insuperable problem, namely that there is no way to make it rational for persons to act morally when they could advance their self-interests by immoral behavior where this immoral behavior would go completely undetected. This was precisely the force of David Gauthier's argument against Kurt Baier.[1] On the other, no society can be a stable one unless

---

[1] See David Gauthier, "Morality and Advantage," *The Philosophical Review* 76 (1967) in which he criticizes Kurt Baier's *The Moral Point of View* (Ithaca: Cornell University Press, 1958). In *Morals by Agreement* (New York: Oxford University Press, 1986), Gauthier tried to ensure stability by introducing the notion of dispositions, the idea being that (a) it can be rational to have a moral disposition and (b) persons do not just change from one position to another. That said, it can be irrational for a person to have one disposition rather than another. If, e.g, a person typically found herself in a position to steal without getting caught, the disposition to refrain from stealing entirely

most of its members refrain from acting immorally in order to advance their self-interests even when they could do so without detection. To be sure, any person is likely to be mistaken in some instances in thinking that her self-interested immoral behavior would go undetected; and this is certainly a reason to be cautious. However, it is surely false that the possibility of being mistaken in some instances makes acting immorally for self-interested purposes irrational for all people in all instances.

Lest it be thought that the argument flounders upon an ambiguity, it should be pointed out that the notion of undetected self-interested immoral behavior can be understood in two ways: (a) no one realizes that a wrong was done; (b) although it is realized that a wrong was done, the actual wrongdoer goes entirely unsuspected. Or, the wrong person is suspected or there are no suspects at all. In either case, however, it will be rational in some instances to suppose that neither form of detection will occur, in which case acting immorally for self-interested purposes will be imminently rational in these instances. Perhaps not for everyone, but surely for enough individuals to undermine the stability of society. And we can even allow that persons are not so driven by self-interests that they will commit a wrongdoing in order to avail themselves of the smallest gain, provided that their wrongdoing will go undetected. If immoral self-interested behavior is confined only to major gains where the behavior will go undetected, the stability of society is still adversely affected in a fundamental way.

could be an irrational one to have. And Gauthier cannot maintain that it would be rational to have a disposition to act morally no matter what else is true, since that stance would essentially leave him open in substance to the very criticism that he raised against Baier.

Of course, it must acknowledge that most people are not that smart or, at least, they are not as reflective as they need to be if they want to act immorally without being detected; hence, it behooves most to act morally even when they think they could get away with acting immorally, since they are more likely to be mistaken than not. Still, none of this shows that life will be shorn of circumstances when it will be quite rational for this or that member of society to act immorally in order to advance her or his self-interests. And there is the rub. Gauthier rightly saw this in criticizing Baier. Ironically, Gauthier's own view, while different from Baier's, does not in the end avoid the very sort of criticism that he raised against Baier. Moreover, while there is always the specter of getting caught, just how bad getting caught is depends upon the penalty levied upon one as well as when one gets caught. For a person who lived a life of crime and who was not caught until she was in the twilight of her years, it is very likely that she lived a more profitable life as an immoral person than she would have lived had she lived a moral life. Or so it is if we are telling the story simply in terms of maximizing self-interests.

Gauthier is generally seen as a modern-day Hobbes, bring-ing to bear the technical apparatus of bargaining theory upon Hobbes's argument. Undoubtedly, the best self-interested argu-ments for morality have their origin in Hobbes's thought. Need-less to say, Rousseau most certainly had read Hobbes; however, Rousseau was deeply unpersuaded by Hobbes's vision of the motivational structure of humanity. In this regard, Rousseau was inspired by the simple, but enormously fecund, observation that holds with equal validity in the state of nature and Civil Society, namely that, first of all, human beings could not survive if the family did not survive; secondly, the family is not one person living alone but a group of individuals with competing interests living together; and thirdly, essential to the survival and stability of the family is the absence of the relentless pursuit of self-interest as the deep motivating feature of persons who are members of the family. What is more, love is at the very center of familial interactions; and love is incompatible with relentless self-interest. The family represents a form of deep interdependence between family members. Its survival and flourishing would be impossible without that interdependence.

Needless to say, the remarks of the preceding paragraph are directly related to the concerns of part 1 of this book. The very idea that human beings are self-interested creatures through and through is in fact incompatible with the very existence of the human race, because it is fundamentally incompatible with the survival of the family. And this is so on two accounts. For one, the marital relationship itself would founder. For another, parenting would be an utter disaster, given the reality that the sentiment of love is a sine qua non for parenting well. Armed with a wealth of technical apparatus, it would seem that moral and political theorists have overlooked the significance of the oldest and most basic of human institutions, namely the family. In the family, cooperation takes place not only between blood-related individuals, namely siblings as well as siblings and parents, but also between two adult individuals who are not related by blood, namely the two parents.

The family would seem to suggest that when self-interest is not at the very fore of human interaction something utterly magnificent can come to pass as a result of human beings interacting. The family reveals the magnificence of interdependence, of the richness that can come about when the relentless pursuit of self-interests takes a back seat to the common goal of having children. Children benefit immeasurably as a result of this joint endeavor on the part of their parents; and anything but this joint parental endeavor shortchanges the children.

Herein lies the key to Rousseau's vision of the transformation that takes place among human beings in the move from the State of Nature to Civil Society: If interdependence between two unrelated individuals can have magnificent results, then might not interdependence among all the members of society also have magnificent results? In the State of Nature families are independent of one another, each family foraging for itself in order to sustain itself. In Civil Society, the families become interdependent. Accordingly, it is only in Civil Society that the artistic, intellectual, and social nature of human beings is realized because the interdependence that relieves each family of the burden of foraging to maintain its basic needs brings forth the talents of individuals, as well as the mutual support of individuals in realizing their talents. It is society as family that elevates humanity. On the one hand, society affords each of its members the liberty to realize their artistic and intellectual nature. On the other, society affords its members the inspiration for such realization either through examples from the other members of society or through their encouragement and admiration.

Much of political theory gives the impression that human beings have no need of one another except in order to address their basic needs. If, for instance, animals could be counted upon to lay food at the feet of human beings and to protect human beings adequately, then to a large extent human beings would be expendable. Human beings provide a service, as it were, and have little or no value in the absence of doing that. This, however, downplays considerably what is distinctive about human beings. They are not just living creatures, but living creatures who possess moral personhood. And the affirmation of moral personhood can no more be reduced merely to providing a service than can parental love for children be so understood.

2 MORAL PERSONHOOD

What is moral personhood? Very succinctly, it is the significance that attaches to (a) the recognition that one has the capacity to value oneself and to express value toward things and other persons is an inescapable feature of one's humanity and (b) the recognition that one can be the object of the expression of value on the part of other beings with moral personhood. Moral personhood involves, at once, both a strength and a vulnerability. The strength, of course, lies in the fact that value can be expressed toward both others and oneself. The vulnerability lies in the fact that one cannot escape being the object of the expression of value that others have toward one, whether that expression of value is positive or negative. Derisive name-calling hurts precisely because such a thing necessarily involves an expression of value. And no matter how rightly and positively we think of ourselves, that assessment cannot be a substitute for the positive assessment of others. Or, from the other direction, our own assessment that what we have done is absolutely ridiculous is rarely, if ever, as painful as a like assessment by someone else who is in the position to judge the success of what we have done.

It may be true, as Kant and Kantians claim, that human beings have intrinsic worth. All the same, we need the affirmation of our intrinsic worth from other human beings, along with the capacity to recognize that the same holds for other human beings. Consider the following: Any person can indeed know that he played a concerto masterfully. For instance, he need only to have recorded his playing of the concerto, and then to compare it with other performances of that concerto that are known to be excellent. Just so, this would not render otiose praise and compliments or, for that matter, criticisms from those who are in the position to assess such things. Quite the contrary, a compliment from a Leonard Bernstein or an André Previn would make an enormous difference. Perhaps with God, who has a perfect will, compliments are unnecessary. Not so with mere mortals.

Now, this example is enormously instructive. We can know beyond the shadow of a doubt that we have exhibited an excellence, because we can see that our performance is on par with other performances of the same that have been judged to be excellent. All the same, the assessments of others in the position to judge matter very, very much to us. Why is that? The answer is quite simple: there is no substitute for a judgment that is independent of our own assessment, where that judgment comes from the expression of another's will. This is so whether that assessment is positive or negative. Nothing changes when it comes to the matter of human beings regarding themselves as having intrinsic moral worth. The affirmation of our moral personhood that comes from another self-valuing being has no equal in power. In this respect, human beings inescapably have need of one another in a way that, as Aristotle observed, neither gods nor animals do. (Of course, Aristotle was somewhat mistaken here because some nonhuman animals are very much social creatures. Chimpanzees come quickly to mind.)

In Kantian language, the duty to affirm the moral personhood of individuals might be characterized as the duty to show persons the proper moral respect. Unfortunately, this way of characterizing things misses the mark because it does not reflect the reality that human beings *need* to be shown the proper moral respect. What is more, there is much in terms of affirmation that is not subsumable under moral duty, as in the case of praise. Praise is profoundly affirming. Yet, the very idea of a moral duty to praise someone quickly borders on the obnoxious. The assertion "I only praised you because I had a moral duty to do so" is most unsatisfying. In fact, it might even be offensive, in that it would be better if the person had said nothing at all than to have uttered that remark. The point here is parallel to the one made regarding parental love in chapter 1 (section 1). Whether or not it can be established that persons have a moral duty to praise others when they exhibit excellences, praise is affirming only when the motivation to do so does not stem from duty. Needless to say, the performative utterance of offering congratulations is a different matter entirely. As is well-known, one can grudgingly congratulate another on winning. This is because in congratulating another, we need not be doing more than merely acknowledging a person's success, which is not at all the same as taking delight in the individual's success.

Having our moral personhood affirmed is not an option that we may take or leave, depending upon how other things are going in our life. This need is a constitutive feature of being a self-valuing creature, although it has nothing to do with staying alive as such, unlike the basic needs. In some sense, this is understandable because much of moral philosophy and political theory concerns itself with the rationality of refraining from harming others. Kantian theory, in particular, is concerned with showing that it is rational to be so moved and that this truth, when human beings are as they should be, determines the effective will of individuals to be so moved.² Let us suppose that the arguments to this effect are entirely sound. From this, it would not thereby follow that it is a constitutive feature of human beings that they need to have their moral personhood affirmed. That one ought to perform an act or has a hard obligation to do so, does not entail that the beneficiary of the behavior in question needs one to so behave. Rousseau did not deny the importance of others behaving as they morally should behave. What is distinctive about him is that he recognized the moral and psychological importance of that behavior to those who are the beneficiaries of it. Even if, as a Thrasymachus of Plato's *Republic* would argue, morality is only for the weak, the affirmation of moral personhood remains of the utmost importance to all. The exception presumably is God, who is perfect in all respects.

To be sure, we must certainly allow that, as self-valuing creatures, human beings pursue things that are in their interest. The point rather is that one misses the mark in characterizing what

---

² See, among others, Stephen Darwall, *Impartial Ethics* (Cornell University Press, 1983); Barbara Herman, *The Practice of Moral Judgment* (Harvard University Press, 1993), and Christine Korsgaard, *The Structure of Normativity* (Cambridge University Press, 1996). Kantians further insist upon the importance of rational creatures having a certain view of themselves. See, for example, Thomas Hill Jr., *Autonomy and Self-Respect* (Cambridge University Press, 1991) and *Human Welfare and Moral Worth* (Oxford University Press, 2002). Needless to say, I certainly accept the view that persons are rationally justified in seeing themselves as having intrinsic moral worth as members of the Kingdom of Ends or as legislators of universal moral law. It is just that I do not see that rational justification entails psychological conviction. For a conception of the self that resonates very much with me, see J. L. A. Garcia's extremely rich essay, "Three Sites for Racism: Social Structures, Valuing, and Vice," in Michael P. Levin and Tamas Pataki (eds.), *Racism in Mind* (Ithaca, NY: Cornell University Press, 2004).

142 ∽ *The Crucible of Society*

it means to be a self-evaluating creature if one fixes upon this while ignoring the fact that qualitative assessment plays a fundamental role in their lives. The judgment concerning how much of a good that one has or even how much of it one has vis à vis another is a quantitative one. By contrast, the judgment that it is worthwhile having the good in question or having as much of it as others is a qualitative one. And this latter kind of judgment is a defining feature of self-evaluating creatures, precisely because it is this judgment that animates them. They do not just act to satisfy their desires; rather, they act with the judgment that doing so is worthwhile, however mistaken that judgment may be. Even the most basic bodily functions are not an exception here, as we understand their importance to living. The judgment that a piece of behavior is worthwhile sometimes yields the conclusion that we ought to perform that behavior although the behavior in question is not itself pleasurable. Thus, human beings sometimes freely engage in behaviors that they know to be unpleasant. It would be quite odd to find an animal freely engaging in a piece of behavior that was causing it enormous pain. This would be proof par excellence that the animal is deranged. By contrast, because human beings are self-evaluators, they can tell a story, which establishes that rather painful behavior on their part can nonetheless be choice-worthy.

Rational choice theorists attempt to finesse the reality that human beings are self-evaluators, and therefore are creatures for whom the judgment of worthiness plays a central role, by making it a defining feature of rationality that in general one would prefer more rather than less of anything deemed to be a good. This move works well for many basic goods, because the judgment that they are worthwhile can certainly be taken for granted. But there are two problems here. One is that the judgment that it would always be rational to prefer more than less of a basic good holds only under very special circumstances, namely ignorance about one's own resources and uncertainty about what the future holds. The other is that life generally presents a plethora of goods all of which no one human being could possibly pursue. Moreover, many goods are incommensurable. As to the first, when people are clear about their own status with respect to the basic needs, rationality as such does not require that individuals still want more rather than fewer things. As to the second, the only way to make choice rational when faced with the option of more goods than one could ever hope to pursue is to invoke a conception of worthiness whereby a choice is made.

Now, it is because human beings are necessarily self-evaluators that they are necessarily concerned with whether or not their actions are choice worthy. And it is the existence of this concern on the part of every reasonable human being that gives rise to interdependence among human beings. The fact that human beings are self-evaluators also explains why the move from the State of Nature to Civil Society is so transforming. This is because Civil Society awakens the affective sentiments, which in turn is tied to being an environment that allows us to pursue ends that are choice worthy and to the affirmation that we receive from others that our ends are choice worthy. The brilliance of Rousseau lies in his grasping the truth that environment alone could make such a drastic difference. This is worth illustrating, as I aim to do in what follows.

3 COMMUNITY AND MORAL PERSONHOOD

Consider the difference that the presumption of safety in a neighborhood makes in how the members of a community go about living their lives on a daily basis. In a community that is plagued by crime, there is fear and dread in the community that is simply not possible in a community that knows little or no crime. In a crime-ridden community, there can be no such things as carefree strolls by adults to take in some fresh air or to enjoy one another's company, as that is tantamount to putting one's life at risk. The well-being of children has to be a concern at every turn, even in broad daylight. They may certainly not walk to and from school without running a very high risk of being harmed in some horrendous way. Nor may they enjoy the outdoor frolicking that is one of the hallmarks of being a child. Doors and windows must be kept locked; and a mere slip in this regard invariably proves costly. In sum, people are prisoners in their own homes. Then there is the fact that so little seems worthwhile doing because it will either be torn down or go radically unappreciated. So a beautiful garden goes unplanted and a lovely playground goes without being built. These are the tangible factors.

Let us also not lose sight of the intangible factors, which are no less substantial. If children cannot play and frolic together, then they miss out on all the richness that comes with doing so, such as the friendships formed and the learning acquired. And if adults cannot stroll along in the evening from time to time, then they miss out on those inspirational moments that only a sunset or a cool breeze against the face can bring. They miss out on the chance encounters with a friend or an acquaintance or perhaps a stranger that give a moment meaning if only because the encounter calls to mind a previous magnificent moment. In a crime-ridden environment, mortifying indifference prevails among far too many members of the community. In general, exhilaration is not occasioned by fear for one's well-being at the hands of others. (So risky activities such as mountain climbing or bungee jumping do not present a problem for these remarks.)

Now whatever else is true, we clearly have considerably less acknowledgement of the moral personhood of persons in a crime-ridden community and considerably more acknowledgement of this in a community that is not crime-ridden. More precisely, there is a direct correlation here; so, it is not as if things could be the other way around. Hence, we have a simple but nonetheless extremely vivid illustration of the favorable difference that comes about in virtue of the moral personhood of individuals being roundly acknowledged. Essentially, the difference amounts to determining a way-of-being for individuals as members of society. The absence of the acknowledgement of moral personhood determines one way-of-being for the members of society, which I shall call the diminutive way, whereas the presence of this acknowledgment determines an entirely different way-of-being for society's members, which I shall call the flourishing way.

We need not determine whether a crime-ridden community is parallel to the state of nature. If things are much worse in the state of nature, that only strengthens the arguement. What is worth noting is the extraordinary difference that the presumption of safety alone makes, where this safety is anchored in none other than mutual respect for the physical well-being of one another. All go about their daily activities with the deep and abiding conviction that others do not have as their aim his or her harm, to be contrasted with people wanting to harm others but having numerous impediments in their way. The absence of harm, then, is owing to the virtue of self-command. All of this entails two things. One is each has the understanding that there is minimum goodwill on the part of all. The other is each has the judgment that she or he is justified in having basic trust in others.

Notice that the sense of safety that I have described is not something that an individual can give himself. For what has been described is an environment of safety as opposed to a situation in which a person has successfully managed to protect herself from the dangers of an environment. Clearly, it is wonderful that an individual can protect herself from the dangers of an environment. That said, it is yet even more wonderful that an individual has no need to so protect herself because her environment is safe. The fact that a person can offer herself protection from the woes of a social environment must not be confused with the fact that a social environment in which she needs no protection can only be offered to her by others.

Now, in view of what the mere assumption of safety entails, suppose that we add the following: any action of merit witnessed would elicit praise and compliments, not only from friends and associates but from various strangers as well. Against the backdrop of safety, this assumption is not particularly difficult to come by. For the minimum goodwill that I have just described, coupled with the conviction of basic trust in others, warrants a measure of gratitude toward the members of society generally; and wherever we have gratitude toward others,[3] displays of excellence

---

[3] My discussion of gratitude here and throughout this chapter owes much to Claudia Card, "Gratitude and Obligation," *American Philosophical Quarterly* 25 (1988) and Terrance McConnell's work *Gratitude* (Temple University Press, 1993). From the standpoint of philosophical psychology, Aaron Ben-Ze'ev masterfully speaks to the subtlety of gratitude. See his *The Subtlety of Emotions* (Cambridge, MA: MIT Press, 2000). See, e.g., ch. 14 "The Sweetest Emotions." Ben-Ze'ev's work persuaded me to focus on gratitude rather than, say, loyalty. He writes: "Gratitude comprises two basic desires: the desire to reward the object personally and the desire for the object's positive evaluation of us"

on their part elicit admiration and praise on our part. Actually the gratitude is manifold. This is because we are not only grateful that our own well-being is secure, which is no trivial matter, but we are also grateful that the well-being of our children is secure, as well as that of our spouse. Arguably, many parents attach more importance to the well-being of their children than to their own well-being. So a society in which the well-being of children is secured makes an enormous difference for the better in terms of the prevailing social climate. We are also grateful for the praise and compliments that are forthcoming from others in response to the excellences exhibited by our children.

At this juncture, it might seem that I have sketched a story that is utterly implausible. In particular, it might seem that the very nature of human beings suggests a much less idyllic outcome. It is, in fact, not uncommon for the individuals to point to the long and veritable seamless history of violence among human beings as proof par excellence that human beings have a wicked nature. Accordingly, there is no reason to think that a society in which safety prevailed would *not* quickly become one in which evil prevailed, as one human being after another exploited the presumption of safety.

The preceding remarks invite the following question: Does social environment make a fundamental difference in terms

(p. 427). Part of gratitude's subtlety lies in the fact that its ubiquity does not at all render it meaningless. See Michael Stocker, "Values and Purposes: The Limits of Teleology and the Ends of Friendship," *The Journal of Philosophy* 78 (1981). In addition, I chose gratitude because I wanted a sentiment that cannot be construed as negative, whatever its value might be. In this regard, see Ruwen Ogien's trenchant discussion of shame in his *La honte est-elle immorale* (Paris: Bayard, 2002).

of the kinds of sentiments that are called for in the lives of individuals? I shall argue that it does.

To begin with, from the viciousness and self-centeredness that regularly occur in an unjust society, we should not infer that it is in the nature of human beings to be vicious and self-centered, regardless of the circumstances in which they find themselves. That would be like supposing that because people in concentration camps would consume morsels of food out of a filthy garbage can that people are naturally inclined to search for food in filthy garbage cans. The same holds if we go in the reverse direction. People who have been well-fed all their lives would not go near a garbage can for food. In the face of starvation, though, these very same people are likely to do just that. None of this shows that there is no human nature. Rather, the conclusion to be drawn is that how human nature manifests itself is inextricably tied to the stability of the kind of environment in which human beings find themselves. Notice that from an evolutionary perspective, a trait of character that manifests itself no matter what is rarely advantageous. Contrary to what one might think, viciousness and self-centeredness are not the exception. For instance, among powerful people of genuine goodwill who do not tolerate wrongdoing, viciousness and self-centeredness would certainly be to a person's disadvantage. Imagine, for instance, that these folks of goodwill would excommunicate such a person rather than put up with his constant attempts to exploit them. With a few simple assumptions, it is easy to see how this could result in this vicious and self-centered person being worse off. For if we now suppose that this person finds himself among others like himself, it turns out that the pay-off for being vicious and self-centered among others like him is considerably less than the pay-off of not being either among people of goodwill.

The history of hostile comportment among human beings may reveal nothing other than that human beings have generally found themselves in rather deplorable social circumstances. Indeed, Rousseau alluded to this himself when he noted that although human beings are born free, they find themselves everywhere in chains. Needless to say, from the fact that deplorable circumstances generally give rise to considerable hostile behavior on the part of individuals, we are surely not warranted in inferring that human beings are naturally inclined to act hostilely toward one another, and thus are inclined so to behave regardless of the social circumstances in which they find themselves. The moral ideal, of course, is that people should behave in the morally right way regardless of the character of the social circumstances in which they find themselves. The moral reality, however, may be that when it comes to morally right behavior, people are more influenced by the character of their social circumstances than no doubt they themselves are either inclined to admit or even willing to believe.

If this is so, then it is with more poignancy than most of us would imagine that evil begets evil. There is nothing mysterious here. For it is not so much that people are eager to do evil and, alas, an evil environment gives them the license so to behave. Rather, it is that if nothing else, an evil environment generally diminishes our resolve to behave morally by, among other things, diminishing the cognitive saliency that the difference between right and wrong behavior has to us. After all, those who act immorally are rarely, if ever, under the impression that they did something other than the immoral act that they in fact committed. Those who maintain their resolve typically do so by affiliating themselves with institutions, especially religious ones, that challenge the evil social environment itself. It is the very rare person who, in the absence of such affiliation, maintains her or his resolve to do what is right notwithstanding the evil that surrounds the individual. In fact, when a community of individuals is surrounded by wrongdoing on all sides, we are impressed that the citizens of that single community should find the resolve to do what is right. That is why the people of Le Chambon have left such a favorable and indelible impression upon us.[4] For this community of people was steadfast in its resolve to save the lives of many Jews notwithstanding the might of the Nazi army, nor the reality that communities all around them bowed to that might or actually welcomed the opportunity to turn Jews over to the Nazis.

To see the plausibility of the claim that the kind of community drastically shapes the kinds of sentiments that are called forth, let us begin, in the spirit of Plato, by looking at things on a smaller scale. Let us consider two radically different social communities in which a child with a loving family is raised. In the one, it is only in the family that the child can count upon and routinely experiences goodwill from others. Let's refer to this community as the Reinmuth community. Outside of the family, the child in the Reinmuth community must always be skeptical of there being genuine goodwill on the part of others, whether they be adults or children. It is typically more reasonable to suppose that there is an ulterior motive behind actions that appear to be gracious and giving, and that even children are most likely to have been put up to no good by their parents. So trusting non-family members

---

4 See Philip Hallie, *Lest Innocent Blood be Shed: The Story of the Village of Le Chambon and How Goodness Happened There* (New York: Harper & Row, 1979). I have tried to shed some further light on this extraordinarily rich moment in *Vessels of Evil: American Slavery and the Holocaust* (Philadelphia, PA: Temple University Press, 1993).

invariably proves to be a mistake on the child's part. This is what the child's parents teach him; and this lesson is borne out by the child's own experiences. In the Reinmuth community, anxiety toward and fear of nonfamily members are an unavoidable part of the child's life.

The Reinmuth community is to be contrasted with the Zwicky community, where things are exactly the opposite. Goodwill abounds. And this is so in two important respects. Oftentimes, the child will have the experience of others being concerned to help him. However, even when this positive manifestation of goodwill is absent, the child discovers that few, if any, even have as their aim to harm him. Thus, the child comes to learn that it is not by happenstance but by design that he can go about his daily activities without having to worry about others wishing to harm him. Not surprisingly, the Zwicky community elicits nothing but trust on the part of the child toward members of the community.

In one community, deep distrust on the part of the child toward non-family members is elicited; whereas in the other, deep trust is elicited. However, putting the point this way considerably under-states the case. In the Zwicky community, it is not clear how a psychologically healthy child could come to have anything but an abiding sense of trust toward non-family members; and in the Reinmuth one, it is not clear how a psychologically healthy child could come to have anything but an abiding sense of distrust toward non-family members. To be sure, a quite unusual story might be applicable in either case that would explain things turning out otherwise. That, though, is just the point. A quite unusual story would be necessary in order to make sense of things turning out otherwise. What is more, no one would think to argue, and it would be utterly absurd to argue, that distrust should be the natural outcome in both the Zwicky and Reinmuth communities, because distrust in the Reinmuth community is very much the rational thing to do or because human beings are naturally self-interested creatures. The manifest reasonableness of trust on the child's part in the Zwicky community is not in any way defeated by the fact that distrust is manifestly reasonable in the Reinmuth community.

Needless to say, though, it is not just that trust would be elicited on the part of the child, but also feelings of goodwill toward members of the community. This is because genuine trust is inescapably tied to the conviction that those trusted care about us. Accordingly, the more the trust pertains to the specificity of a person's life (as opposed to basic human concerns), the more those who are trusted in this are thought to care. It would take a very complicated explanation to make sense of a child who detested the members of her community, though the child took them to care deeply about her well-being.

The preceding remarks regarding a child are readily acknowledged and accepted by all. The fact of the matter, however, is that these remarks hold for adults. This is especially true of adults living in a Zwicky-like community, who as children were also raised in a Zwicky-like community. For this results in what we might call positive dispositional continuity between the developmental and the mature stages of the self. In the absence of some extraordinary aberration, no psychologically healthy individual raised in a Zwicky-like environment as a child and living in one as an adult would be disposed to be distrusting of the members of the community or to have hostile sentiments toward them. By contrast, if we take a person who had been raised and who had matured in a Reinmuth-like community (thereby resulting in negative dispositional continuity) and place him into a Zwicky-like one, then we can readily make sense of his suspicions and hostilities. In fact, we can even make sense of these sentiments enduring on the person's part, although they are surely unwarranted, because we know that the systematic mistreatment of a child can scar the individual for life. Yet, these considerations, far from suggesting the absence of human nature, indicate that how human nature manifests itself is ineluctably tied to the character of the social environment in which human beings find themselves.

Let us take note of where we have arrived. We have seen the difference that merely the assumption of safety makes as a vehicle for affirming the moral personhood of individuals, along with the enormous difference this makes in terms of creating an abundance of opportunities for the lives of persons to be enriched. And we have just drawn attention to the obvious point that a child raised in a warm environment will be disposed to be trusting of others. Together, these two points speak to the raison d'être of this book. The trajectory of human life begins with childhood rather than adulthood. Necessarily, a climate of safety and trust among the adults of a society would produce trusting children who would take their turn as adults who sustained the society's climate of safety and trust. To be sure, the cycle of goodness, if you will, can be broken. Things can go awry. That said, we must not lose sight of the truth that there is no account of human nature available which makes it reasonable to expect that children raised in an environment of warmth and trust will become vicious and hostile on account of that environment itself. Thus, children raised in an environment of warmth and trust are favored to become adults who affirm the moral personhood of one another, as a result of which we have an environment that creates opportunities for the lives of persons to be enormously enriched. Notice, though, that on this account, self-interest is not the modus operandi of society. Far from it. Rather, it is the trust that individuals have in one another. Yet, a society in which trust prevails turns out to be very much in everyone's self-interest.

I believe that part of the genius of Rousseau lies in his presupposing, without having the theoretical machinery at hand to underwrite his thought, that human nature does not manifest itself in the same way under radically different conditions. For Rousseau, contract theory was never about finding a way for human beings to live together despite their unalterable wicked human nature, but about articulating a conception of living together that gives rise to an entirely different aspect of human nature. In this respect, Rousseau echoes Aristotle's thought that human beings are not good or bad by nature. This reality does not in the least show that goodwill would fail to be a part of the very fabric of the moral character of all human beings were they in an environment that wondrously affirmed their moral personhood. Nor, interestingly, does it follow that the very idea of human nature must be abandoned if we allow that whether human beings are disposed to display goodwill or ill-will is mightily influenced by their social environment.

What might have inclined Rousseau to perceive that human nature does not manifest itself in the same way under radically different conditions? The answer is the family itself. For no one would think, and certainly Rousseau did not suppose, that the character of the family environment was irrelevant to the kind of adult that a child turned out to be. Language also stands as an indisputable example of the fact that environment makes a difference.[5] Every human being's first language is inextricably

---

[5] Rousseau, of course, had lots of very interesting things to say about language in his work *Essai sur l'Origine des Langues.* For instance, he held in chapter 2 that although the basic needs gave rise to gestures, it is the passions that gave

tied to the social community in which she or he was raised; and all human beings are such that were they raised in a different social environment they would speak with just as much mastery the language common to that environment. Yet, from none of this does it follow that there is no human nature. The case of language is particularly instructive because it is not possible for a psychologically and physically healthy person not to master the language of the social community in which she or he is raised. Even if individuals should go on to master another language as well, they are favored to master, first of all, the language of their social community. A special explanation is required in order to make sense of a person mastering a different language first.

4 SOCIAL UNITY AND THE AFFECTIVE SENTIMENTS

Emotions or feelings are not unique to human beings. Fear and anger are two very powerful emotions, both of which are exhibited by many nonhuman animals. And it is equally clear that some animals can have feelings of trust. However, these feelings are primarily tied to a binary function: harm or not harm. What they do not involve, in any case, are assessments of character. Assessments of character are not only tied to what a person does, but to what was available to him and to whether or not there are satisfactory explanations for why the individual failed to behave in a certain way. Take for example a dog that is continually well fed. The dog does not really care that the meat being given to him is not the best cut available in the home or is not as good

---

rise to language. Without debating whether Rousseau got this right, two points are worth mentioning. One is that we often suppose that we can determine what the needs of animals are by their behavior. The other is that we do not attribute to animals the passions that we attribute to human beings.

as the cut one is eating. It does not even matter that the only meat one gives the dog is the meat one could not finish eating on one's plate. On the other hand, if fate should have it that one is no longer able to feed the dog, whatever the dog does will not be based upon the dog's assessment of whether or not any excusing conditions obtain. Again, while it can be made clear to dogs that certain behavior will result in them experiencing an undesirable reaction, they do not assess whether the limitations imposed are reasonable or not. No dog is thinking for instance "I understand that urinating in the house is inappropriate, but I cannot for the life of me see why I cannot lie on the living room couch." More generally, praise and blame are not a part of the life of animals, at least not in any robust sense that would incline us to assess dogs morally.[6]

Needless to say, it is a different matter entirely with human beings. Incontrovertibly, human beings are capable of the affective sentiments; and this goes hand in hand with the capacity of human beings to make moral judgments. My thesis in this final section can be put quite simply as follows: When the affective sentiments are as they should be among the members of society, then society thereby provides a most ennobling environment. The proviso, of course, is that things have gone the way they should in the family.

When things go as they should in the family, children are encouraged to develop their talents. Children are admired and praised for the excellences that they exhibit; and criticisms come

---

[6] On this see, Aaron Ben-Ze'ev, *op. cit.*, p. 107ff. Ronald de Sousa, *Évolution et rationalité* (Paris: Presses Universitaires de France, 2004), notes that although Aristotle attributed to animals the capacity for syllogistic reasoning, they are not capable of theoretical reasoning. See pp. 126–8.

in a constructive and supportive way. Indeed, the very point of punishing a child is not to make her or him worse off, but to teach the child an important lesson. In all of this, a wealth of sentiments is involved. These affective sentiments are absolutely crucial to the effectiveness of either praise or criticism and punishment. As I have already indicated, praise without the appropriate affective sentiments fails to be affirming. By contrast, criticism and punishment without the appropriate affective sentiments are apt to come across as mean-spirited. So much of this is obvious. Far from obvious, however, is that a similar claim can be made regarding society. I shall illustrate this in a rather usual way by taking up the case of gratitude. Why I have done so shall become clear as we proceed.

Gratitude is conceptually tied to the belief – the cognitive assessment – that another has acted with goodwill on one's behalf. A person would have to be either evil or schizophrenic were he to recognize that another had acted with goodwill on his behalf and yet this recognition did not figure positively into his motivations with regard to that person. Thus, Frederic Douglass maintained that nothing reminded him more of the infernal character of slavery than the base ingratitude of slaveowners toward the slaves who worked loyally and faithfully for them.[7] We might imagine that Douglass reasoned as follows: Even if slaveowners viewed slaves as inferior, the owners ought to have been moved by the loyalty and faithfulness of their slaves that manifested itself in the slaves lovingly caring for the children of the slaveowners; and the fact that the owners were not so moved

---

[7] Here I am following Michael Stocker's "The Schizophrenia of Modern Ethical Theories," *The Journal of Philosophy* 73 (1973). See also my "Gratitude and Social Equality," *The Hedgehog Review* 3 (2001).

serves to reveal how wicked they and the institution of slavery were. It is a striking fact about gratitude that one cannot express gratitude toward another without taking that person seriously. So contrary to what many have supposed, Douglass was right to single out the absence of gratitude as a more profound measure of the evil of slavery than the physical violence of slavery itself. This is because the absence of physical violence can be tied to factors, such as costs, that have nothing whatsoever to do with taking another seriously; but not so with gratitude.[8] These remarks also explain why it is true that sometimes in life, we want another's gratitude more than just about anything else. Or gratitude, while not necessarily making things right, may nonetheless make the wrongs less unbearable. Typically, parents who have raised their children do not want anything in return from their children but their children's gratitude. And although gratitude toward the slaves who cared for the slaveowners' children would not have made slavery itself any less wrong, it would nonetheless have had a most salubrious effect upon the very souls of those who gave of themselves in this way.

Although I shall not argue the case here, I think that what is taken to be gratitude toward animals is properly understood as satisfaction in their behavior. Gratitude entails satisfaction in the way another behaved, but the reverse is not true. If Jones owns lots of jewelry and Smith swam through shark-infested waters in order to save Jones's life, it would make perfectly good sense to anyone that Jones sells some of his jewelry in order to buy a spectacular gift to show his gratitude toward Smith. Suppose,

---

[8] I should like to think that these remarks are consistent with Charles Mills, *The Racial Contract* (Ithaca, NY: Cornell University Press, 1997).

though, that instead of Smith it was Jones's dog, Rusty, that saved him. We would expect Jones to hug and pet Rusty profusely. But suppose that Jones announced that he was selling some of his jewelry to do something spectacular for Rusty. This would surely strike us as going too far. Now, what is the difference between Smith saving Jones from shark-infested waters and Rusty doing so? The answer is that Smith fully grasps the moral significance of what she is doing. Dogs can recognize danger and that others are in danger. From this, however, it does not follow that dogs grasp the moral significance of saving someone from danger. This observation allows us another way to see the depth of Douglass's remarks about slavery. What he must have surely grasped is that gratitude carries in its wake the recognition of another's moral personhood.

Before moving on, I wish to draw attention to the fact that it is possible to have gratitude toward a person, although the person has done for one that which she or he was obligated to do on one's behalf. Obligations can be fulfilled begrudgingly or with enormous goodwill. A professor, for example, may reluctantly give the student the "A" he deserves, because the student was slothful and arrogant. Or, she may do so with joy because the student, owing to some initial tutoring from her, so remarkably overcame a huge intellectual deficit and rightly earned his place among the very best students. Although the student earned the "A," he recognizes that this reality is owing in large measure to the dedication of his professor and her commitment to his succeeding. Her commitment to his succeeding went beyond the call of duty; and for that commitment on her part, he is forever grateful. It does not matter whether the duty in question is purely a moral one, or is one that is institutionally defined. Or, to take another example, by paying back the money that he borrowed from Aziz, Smith did what was his moral duty. Yet, Smith did this so graciously that Aziz is moved and grateful to Smith.

Now, in a just society, gratitude is a sentiment that is naturally continuous with the transition from childhood to adulthood. Children are naturally grateful to their parents for the love and support that has been given to them by their parents. In terms of its structure, there is no difference at all between the gratitude that we have here and the gratitude that a person naturally has toward a stranger who saves his life. In general, the structure of gratitude is the same, although its expression may vary across cultures and between different levels of social standing. Here is an example that illustrates the latter. Hugging one's parents as an expression of gratitude for the new house they gave one would rarely be inappropriate. Hugging the Queen of England, by contrast, would be another matter entirely, although a new house is precisely what was received from her as well. The structure of gratitude is the same, although its expression is not.

In addition to being continuous with the transition from childhood to adulthood, it is also the case that gratitude may help us to understand the significance of a form of patriotism that has no morally obnoxious overtones. Gratitude acknowledges the good that has been done on one's behalf without thereby diminishing others. If Jamilla saved José from drowning, then his gratitude toward her will not at all involve thinking less of those who did not. Thinking less of others would be appropriate only if José had independent grounds for believing that others desired his harm. Further, one can be equally grateful to more than one person, because gratitude is not depleted by its expression. If together, Jamilla and Natasha worked equally hard in order to save José's life, he does not in any way have to choose between them when it comes to expressing his gratitude. In this respect, gratitude is like parental love. Equally noteworthy is the fact that gratitude, like love, cannot be coerced.

If patriotism is founded in gratitude, then it need not embody a superior mindset toward other nations.[9] One can have gratitude toward one's own nation without thinking less of other nations, just as one can have gratitude toward one's own family without thinking for a moment that the other families have to be worse than one's own. Quite the contrary, gratitude in this regard is enormously compatible with admiration for other nations or families, as the case may be. We are profoundly shaped by our family and our nation; and when this is for the better, gratitude is certainly appropriate. Finally, in this connection the following should be said. There is nothing about gratitude that implies an uncritical acceptance of the other. This holds for gratitude with respect to parents. So, a fortiori, it holds for gratitude with respect to our nation. Hence, patriotism anchored in gratitude is not, in the nature of things, aligned with the obnoxious patriotism of uncritical acceptance demanded by a totalitarian regime. Uncritical acceptance is not even an initial sign of gratitude. It is, instead, a sign of subservience. No more; no less. Patriotism most certainly can be something of which a person should be ashamed. But it should be borne in mind that this does not follow from the nature of patriotism itself. If we can have good reason to be grateful to our nation, then we can very well have good reason to be patriotic.

Now gratitude is a marvelous lubricant of social interaction. This is because gratitude is a particularly personal affirmation

---

[9] I am indebted here to Alasdair MacIntyre's 1984 Lindley Lecture, "Is Patriotism a Virtue?"

of the moral power that a person possesses to make a difference for the better in the life of another and, most importantly, of the reality that she has thus used her moral power. Accordingly, being the object of gratitude elevates us without disposing us to be arrogant, because it necessarily requires that we take seriously the person who expresses it. Gratitude is a lubricant of social interaction because it disposes us either to do more good for the same person or to do good for others, or even to repeat the same good for the same person on a later occasion. When people are profoundly grateful, they can be remarkably creative in finding ways to express their gratitude. There is almost always something that one can do.

A rather significant fact in this regard is that expressions of gratitude need not be costly at all. Likewise, they are rarely about giving people what they need in order to survive. Rather, they need only reflect the reality that one did something for the person in which she or he would take delight. As an expression of gratitude, it may be that the person went out of his way to find a special item that we always wanted but never had enough time or patience to look for, or perhaps we were never in the right location. Or, by contrast, perhaps the individual is known for his sewing abilities and he made us the silk vest that we have always wanted. The cost of the material was about $70; but the gift of the vest is priceless. After all, many things that have enormous sentimental value for us are things that we could have easily purchased ourselves. Gratitude at its best transforms the object that is given because the object is symbolic of the desire to do a good, namely to produce an object that is particularly meaningful to the recipient at a personal level. This certainly can involve speaking to a very present need. But as I noted at the outset, this is often not the case. Friends are often marvelous at this sort of thing. This, I believe, is one reason why complete or companion friendship, as Aristotle conceived of it, is so precious.[10]

I hold that the real measure of equality in a society, across differences, is not so much that the percentage of people in various positions accords with the percentage of their numbers in the general population. Rather, it is when there are genuine expressions of gratitude across differences. No less significant is the fact that we often want to repay people for their expressions of gratitude. Ingratitude, by contrast, is essentially an affront to our goodwill; and its persistence can incline even the most determined to retreat. To be sure, no decent person helps another who is drowning, say, in order to be the object of that individual's gratitude. Just so, even the most saintly do not want the good that they do denied or discounted. Thus, gratitude is important to even the saintly.

When things proceed as they should, the first lessons of gratitude are taught to children by their parents, as the parents express delight in the small gestures of affection and love that their children display toward them. I have highlighted this in order to draw attention to the reality that there is nothing about gratitude that makes it appropriate only when a person has done

[10] For some of the most important essays on friendship, see Neera Badhwar (ed.), *Friendship: A Philosophical Reader* (Ithaca, NY: Cornell University Press, 1993). See especially her introduction, "The Nature and Significance of Friendship." For my own views regarding friendship, see *Living Morally: A Psychology of Moral Character* (Philadelphia, PA: Temple University Press, 1993), chapters 4 and 5; and my entry "Friendship" in the *Encyclopedia of Applied Ethics* (1998). In her recent work, *Making a Necessity of Virtue: Aristotle and Kant on Virtue* (New York: Cambridge University Press, 1997), Nancy Sherman offers in chapter 5, "The Shared Voyage," a very moving account of the sharing that takes place between friends.

something extraordinary on our behalf or something that we could not have done for ourselves. Indeed, the family shows all too well that much gratitude can be in response to very small things that family members do for one another – things that the family member might have very well done for herself. Thus, suppose that the teenage son has a spell of tidiness, and is moved to clean his room. While taking the trash from his room to the garbage cans outside, he makes a point of emptying the trashcans in the bathrooms and the kitchen. This turns out to be simply a gesture of thoughtfulness on his part in this regard. His parents might be quite appreciative of this, although the son has not performed a task of great moral or social significance. Certainly, he has not done anything that the parents could not do themselves. In addition to the gratitude that parents show their children, there is the gratitude that children witness between their parents. Suppose, for instance, that a husband decides to iron a few of his shirts instead of wearing them straight out of the dryer. While doing this, he also irons two of his wife's uniforms and puts them in the closet. Again, we do not have anything spectacular here. Yet, the wife is brimming with gratitude. She takes them out of the closet and hangs them in a conspicuous spot in the kitchen. When the children ask why she replies "So everyone can see what daddy has done for mommy." That is a lesson in gratitude for the children.

It goes without saying that we should be grateful for the major sacrifices that others make on our behalf or the major risks that they take to secure our well-being. We can be fortunate enough, though, not to be needy in these sorts of ways. Indeed, Aristotle makes just this point about friendship at its best. Yet, nothing would be more stunning if friendship at its best did not involve gratitude. This is because friends typically do for one another small things to convey their affection and appreciation for one another – small things that they did not have to do and that the friend surely could have done for her or himself. Most people will at some point in time receive from a loved-one (family member or friend) a pen set as a gift. With rare exception, most recipients of such a gift can easily purchase the item for themselves. All the same, the gratitude occasioned by such gifts is always enormous. This is because their significance lies in the fact that they serve as marvelous reminders that we were chosen, if you will, to be the object of another's kindness and thoughtfulness.[11] And such reminders always have a most salubrious effect on us. This is the reason why parents have so much gratitude for the little things that their children choose to do for them; for those little things are such extraordinary reminders of the place that parents have in the hearts of their children. In this regard, children serve as a reminder that as a moral power gratitude is rarely beyond the reach of an individual. A family of little means may offer as a gesture of gratitude to the neighbor the special "cake of the house" that everyone in the community raves about, or the family may tend to the neighbor's lawn in the summer or driveway in the winter. And so on.

Bearing the above remarks in mind, then one of the striking things that follows is that we can have gratitude for the self-command that people exercise in acting morally and justly toward us. And this is as it ought to be, precisely because such behavior counts only if it represents the free and deliberate

---

[11] For this way of putting the point, I am indebted to two high school students, Paul Frey and Brian Keevil. Together and independently, each was masterful in showcasing the virtues of autonomy and self-command in expressing their gratitude on occasion, and in indicating why it is important for them to do so.

choice of individuals so to behave. The exercise of self-command in this regard is none other than an affirmation of our moral personhood. And our gratitude returns the compliment. Society is as it should be, surely, when we have this combination of self-command and gratitude. And when we do, what we have is social unity anchored in self-command and gratitude. Thus, if I may hearken back to our remarks regarding patriotism, I merely want to say that we most certainly can have reasons to be grateful for the society in which we live.

I have focused on the affective sentiment of gratitude precisely because, on the one hand, it is a considerable moral power the exercise of which requires so little and because, on the other, it is an appropriate response to what in many ways is mundane but yet ever so appropriate. Politeness, I believe, is a natural outgrowth of an environment that is animated by self-command and gratitude. For politeness can be understood as a social sign of moral respect in the absence of a moral problem that needs to be addressed. Hence, in a just society gratitude is a social lubricant that, in turn, generates another layer of social lubrication. There are dispositional fits.[12] Gratitude and politeness constitute a dispositional fit, as does general ingratitude and the general absence of politeness. It is certainly possible that an individual might have considerable gratitude toward an individual and yet not be disposed to be polite toward that person. This, though, would be most unlikely, requiring a very unusual story. If a neo-Nazi were to find the wherewithal to save a Jew's life, where it is clear to all parties who is whom, then the gratitude on the Jew's part might certainly express itself in a measure of restraint

[12] I introduced this expression in "Ethical Egoism and Psychological Dispositions," *American Philosophical Quarterly* (1980).

vis à vis hostility toward that particular neo-Nazi, because after all he (the Jew) owes his life to him (that neo-Nazi). Without for a moment weakening his opposition to the neo-Nazi ideology, the Jew could, and should, be ever so grateful that the neo-Nazi saved his life.

5 THE BACKDROP OF FLOURISHING

In one sense, flourishing is a very individualistic matter. It would be correct to say that some people are capable of flourishing in the very bowels of hell. Frederic Douglass did; Elie Wiesel did. Harriet Jacobs did as well. I think of black gospel music as yet another instance of flourishing under horrendous circumstances. It is a music that made it possible for a people to have hope when precious little in their environment warranted their having hope. In fact, I hold that forms of idiosyncratic excellence often emerge in the context of evil, as the downtrodden seek to survive and affirm themselves.[13] That said, the reality is that at the individual level most people wither rather than flourish under sustained conditions of evil. Agreeable conditions are a must for all but a very few souls.

In the previous section, I described an agreeable social climate and thus one that is conducive in general to the members of society flourishing. This is because such conditions are conducive to the members of society appreciating the excellences exhibited by one another without regard to the contingencies of either gender or ethnicity or religious convictions or sexual orientation. For where self-command is exercised across the board in society,

---

[13] I am indebted here to Howard McGary, *Race and Social Justice* (Blackwell, 1999). I develop the idea of idiosyncratic excellence in "Equality and the Mantra of Diversity," *The University of Cincinnati Law School* 72 (2004).

then gratitude across the board is also warranted. The viciousness of bias often lies not in the physical harms perpetrated against us, but in the near-immutable conviction that one is incapable of excellence. For when we believe that a person or a people is incapable of excellence, this very belief often disposes us to discount an exhibited excellence in favor of an alternative hypothesis that best fits our low expectations. For instance, admirable determination can be seen as rude insistence. Or whether someone is seen as giving a matter deep thought or as being intellectually slow is more often than not tied to the expectations that one brings to the encounter. Now, imagine a society in which gratitude is widespread among citizens. Of course, adjustments have to be made for the fact that most members of society do not live together and are, in fact, strangers to one another. And it might be thought to follow from this consideration alone that gratitude could not be widespread in society.

People are often discouraged because they have little reason to believe that the good they do will be acknowledged. By contrast, next to self-motivation itself, few things motivate us to pursue excellence more than the knowledge that the excellences we exhibit will be acknowledged and appreciated. Gratitude is one of the forms of acknowledgement and appreciation. In this regard, the difference between gratitude from the general public and gratitude on the part of a family member or a close friend is significant, due not so much to the possibility that there is greater objectivity with the former, although that is a factor, but to the greater psychological independence of the former. Like an arrow already drawn, our friends and loved-ones are poised to acknowledge the excellences we exhibit. They are already loyal members of our fan club, if you will. Not so with members of the general public. Neither category of individuals can replace the other. What we most need sometimes is the support of our family and friends. On other occasions, what would surely make a most dramatic difference to us is an acknowledgement that comes from someone with whom we have no ties.

Now, it will be observed that since the beginning of the preceding section, I have not made any reference to meeting the basic needs. I have not done so in this section, even though its focus is flourishing. If I have understood Rousseau correctly, it is not when the basic needs are met that the soul of humankind is elevated, and the lives of individuals are enriched and ennobled. Rather, it is when and only when the affective sentiments are as they should be. And when this is so, human beings do something that no other group of creatures can do.

Among mammals, there are many creatures that care for their young. One is surprised, at times, to learn just how much attention some mammals give to their young. But none have, because none can have, the intention to make the world a better place for themselves and their young. For it is only in having the wherewithal to get beyond the grip of basic needs that such a realization is possible. When Civil Society is as it should be, however, we have a social environment that achieves this end. And it is only in a social environment such as this that future generations can be given the gift of the possibility of yet a more perfect union. To live *sub species aeternitatis* is to have, and to be animated by, the knowledge that we make the world a better place for the future by living a more perfect life in the present. This we can do only if society is systematically conducive to the elevation of the souls of its citizens. It is only by being one among ourselves that we can have the hope of being one with the future. What is more, anything less than *E Pluribus Unum* is not Civil Society as it should and could be, if it should be called Civil Society at all.

Epilogue

Liberty: Between Plato and Modern Liberalism

M uch of contemporary political theory reads as if the most important good that an individual could possess,[1] given that all basic needs are adequately met, is liberty. To be sure, an immutable constraint is that everyone must have the same liberty; hence, some forms of liberty are ruled out because either not everyone could have that liberty or society would cease to be stable if everyone did. It is striking that Rousseau thought no such thing. For he held that human beings possessed more liberty in the State of Nature than in Civil Society. What is more, he thought that human beings were generally able to meet their basic needs even in the State of Nature, although admittedly Civil Society facilitates that considerably. In the State of Nature human beings have pure liberty, as I shall say. They are free to do whatever it is that they have the wherewithal to do. What Rousseau grasped most profoundly is that pure liberty leaves human beings shorn

---

[1] It is, I believe, one of the great merits of Monique Canto-Sperber's recent work in moral philosophy that it does not privilege liberty above all else. See her recent *L'Inquiètude Morale et la vie humaine* (Paris: Presses Universitaires de France, 2003). This epilogue owes much to that work and to Jean-Fabien Spitz's book *La Liberté Politique* (Paris: Presses Universitaires de France, 1995), especially chapter 8, "Rousseau et la critique de la modernité."

of an awful lot. In particular, it leaves them shorn of the basic ingredients by virtue of which human beings will flourish, where minimally flourishing is understood as using one's talents and gifts in productive ways that make the human condition more ennobling.

I shall contrast pure liberty with what I call structured liberty. In Western thought the most well-known example of structured liberty is Plato's *Republic*, which interestingly Rousseau held to be a most important work. Yet, Rousseau's political writings bear little or no resemblance to Plato's *Republic*. Most of us today admire Plato without thinking for a moment that society should be modeled after his famous account of society. The structured liberty of Plato's *Republic* is best understood as liberty by a priori design or simply a priori liberty. With a priori liberty, the good of the individual is made subordinate to the good of society.

Rousseau sought to steer a course between pure liberty with its shortcomings and a priori liberty with its shortcomings. For nonhuman animals, pure liberty is ideal. This is because there are no excellences characteristic of nonhuman animals that another kind of liberty would occasion and underwrite, where as this is precisely the case with human beings. A priori liberty avoids the problem of pure liberty only by making human beings a means to the end of society itself. Rousseau wanted something weaker. I shall call it anchored liberty, because the liberty is anchored in the capacity for human flourishing. Anchored liberty steers a course between pure and a priori liberty. Presumably Rousseau reasoned as follows: If the good of society should not be placed above the good of the individual, because society should, in fact, serve the good of the individuals in society, then surely a like claim holds for liberty. Rousseau did not think that all forms of liberty were compatible with human beings flourishing – that is, with human beings achieving the excellences of which they are capable. Accordingly, he held that liberty without a sense of direction made human beings rather like animals. The worth of liberty, he supposed, lies in its awakening and nourishing the excellences of which human beings are capable. And the *Social Contract* was written with this vision of liberty in mind.

Thus, Rousseau rejected the view that for human beings liberty is a good in and of itself and, therefore, that society does what is good for its citizens simply by virtue of maximizing their liberty. More precisely, he understood that liberty is no guarantee at all that those who possess it will chose well. Although animals have pure liberty, the issue of choosing unwisely does not arise for them, because their desires and choices are roundly constrained by their make-up. Not so with humans, however. And therein lies the problem. There is nothing about the very nature of human beings that entails that with pure liberty human beings will choose to realize the excellences of which they are capable. Thus for Rousseau society steps in where nature leaves off, not by providing a Platonic-like rigid grid, but by providing a backdrop that would favor human beings making ennobling choices.

Modern liberalism gets much of its force from the supposed truth that there is no conception of the good that society should privilege other than that citizens should not harm one another. Accordingly, if a citizen wants to do no more with her talents than count blades of grass, then that is her choice provided that she neither harms others nor becomes a burden to others. The example comes from Rawls's *A Theory of Justice.* Rawls's counter of blades of grass is quite talented because he supports himself by solving mathematical problems on the side. Thus, he is in fact contributing to the good of others. So with Rawls's blade-of-grass counter, we do not at all have a life shorn of excellence. Rather, we have one in which a well-developed excellence is put to use in a most nonconventional manner, namely to support an activity that would seem to have no point at all. In the end, then, this example hardly supports the modern liberal view that anything a person does is just fine as long as he does not harm anyone and he is not a burden to anyone.

The kind of case that is needed, if modern liberalism is to make its case, is the ferociously independent bum. She loves her whiskey and she keeps herself alive by eating scraps from the restaurants in the neighborhood. Health policies for restaurants ensure that there will always be plenty of scraps. Moreover, restaurants would prefer to give away their scraps to people like her rather than simply to throw the scraps away. Her home is an underpass of a bridge, which always is warm in the winter (owing to heating devices installed to prevent the accumulation of snow and ice) and cool in the summer. She spends her days counting cars – when, that is, she is sober enough to count anything at all. She gets her whiskey money, by the way, by positioning herself in front of a post office and opening the door for persons entering and exiting. On a good day, she can earn as much as $70; and with that money, she was prudent enough, quite some time ago, to buy one of those life insurance policies that excludes coverage for the first two years after acquiring it. Even in death, then, she will not be a burden to anyone. She harms no one and is not a burden to anyone. Now, this is a life shorn of excellence.

The depth of Rousseau's insight can be seen by what I suggest would be his response to the whiskey bum scenario. He would argue, I believe, that a just society is not so much one that provides for people like the whiskey bum, but rather one that is structured so that, in the first place, there would be very few people like the whiskey bum. This is because for the whiskey bum there is very little, if anything, that would recommend Civil Society over the State of Nature, which is to say that society has lost its reason for being. A society that does not roundly disfavor the occurrence of whiskey bums among its citizens violates the first axiom of social contract theory, namely that each member of society should be better off merely on account of being in society. Given the reality that social processes are invariably imperfect, then the idea behind social contract theory is that every individual has good reasons to believe that society is such that the odds are very much against her or his turning out to be anything like a whiskey bum, because liberty is configured in such a way in society that makes this a most unlikely outcome. As Rousseau would conceive of it, then, structured liberty is not as much about limiting liberty as it is about configuring liberty so that certain undesirable outcomes are highly unlikely. Or in other words, liberty would be configured so as to favor excellence and disfavor the nadir of excellence. However, this cannot be done a priori.

Without a doubt what counts as excellent is a very complicated matter. Furthermore, there is constant evolution with regard to the notion. That said, it is better to debate continually what counts as excellence than to hold that the very idea of excellence is entirely empty. And if this is right, then the liberal thought that liberty, with the usual proviso of not causing others harm, is the ultimate good is misguided. More precisely, justice that makes no reference to excellence is justice best applied to animals than to human beings. The best of all worlds would be one in which all human beings delighted in the pursuit of excellence. The next best world is not one that privileges liberty above all else (with the usual proviso concerning harm to others). Rather, it is perhaps one in which people have the liberty to live as they so choose, but the very fabric of society is a gentle, but firm reminder, that the value of liberty for all human beings lies in our choosing to be excellent. Without a doubt, the choice is one that each individual must make for her or himself. This truth, however, is nonetheless compatible with the following two options: In one case, the society in which we live marvelously inspires each of its members to be excellent, where there is no coercion whatsoever. In the other case, it is equally true that there is no coercion whatsoever to live a life of excellence. However, in this latter case, it is deemed that excellence is that which should not speak its name. Rousseau's view, quite simply, is that not only is the former rationally preferable to the latter, because it best accords with what makes human beings different from animals in a fundamentally important way, but also that the former is, in virtue of its configuration, a vastly more stable society. The former is an alternative that lies between Plato's *Republic* and modern liberalism; and it is superior to both. Parents who give birth to children, but then do nothing at all to underwrite each child's flourishing are horrendous parents. A society that valorizes pure liberty, instead of excellence, is no better. For it is not weakness but a reality that we are all better off when the encouragement to be excellent is an inextricable part of the fabric of our lives from start to finish. Rousseau wrote with the hope that human beings would never lose sight of what sets them apart from animals, namely that human beings can make the choice to be excellent. In order for us as humans to live well, it is not enough that we recognize this reality. Rather, we must with grace and purity of heart affirm the capacity for excellence in all at every level of society. Human beings are the only animals who can bestow upon themselves and posterity the gift of excellence. In exchanging pure liberty for anchored liberty, Civil Society is the conduit whereby the gift of excellence is bestowed in perpetuity.

Index

sex act, the
  and wish to bear children, 5
  de-coupled from conception,
    13
sexism, 15, 72
sexual equality
  as equality across differences,
    115–17
  See also multiculturalism
Sherman, Nancy, 163
Shoeman, Ferdinand, 49
Sober, Elliott, 60
social contract theory
  basic idea of, 9, 104
Sowden, Lanning, 125
state of mind
  desirability of vs. acquisition of,
    32
State of Nature. *See* Civil Society
Stinnett, Nick, 86
Stocker, Michael, 24, 147, 157
sub species aeternitatis
  to live, 169

Thomas, Laurence, 8, 15, 21, 27, 40,
  97, 150, 157, 163, 166, 167

Thrasymachus, 67, 141
Tocqueville, Alex de, 27
Trachtenberg, Joshua, 71
Trivers, Robert, 59, 60
trust
  and care, 152
  importance of, 100, 153

Ulysses, 128
Uncle Tom, 26

Velleman, J. David, 20, 91

Walker, James, 86
Wallace, George, 97, 99
wanted-out-of-love stance,
  14–16
Watson, Gary, 40
Wiesel, Elie, 167
Williams, Bernard, 24

zero-sum
  parental love vs. familial
    resources, 113
  See also parental love,
    fellow-feeling